Olivier Theyskens

She walks in beauty

Rizzoli Electa

She walks in beauty, like the night
Of cloudless climes and starry skies;
And all that's best of dark and bright
Meet in her aspect and her eyes:
Thus mellow'd to that tender light
Which heaven to gaudy day denies.

One shade the more, one ray the less,
Had half impaired the nameless grace
Which waves in every raven tress,
Or softly lightens o'er her face;
Where thoughts serenely sweet express
How pure, how dear their dwelling-place.

And on that cheek, and o'er that brow,
So soft, so calm, yet eloquent,
The smiles that win, the tints that glow,
But tell of days in goodness spent,
A mind at peace with all below,
A heart who's love is innocent!

Lord Byron, 1813

FOREWORD

In 1997, when Olivier Theyskens took his first steps in fashion and launched his own fashion house, he was a fresh young twenty-year-old who had prematurely quit his studies in fashion at the La Cambre school in Brussels. Twenty years later, having been in fashion for half his life, he can look back on an impressive career with a most exceptional trajectory. Theyskens belongs to the second generation of Belgian designers, those who made international names for themselves at the end of the twentieth century. Characteristic of this second generation was the speed with which its primarily very young designer members made their names on the world's fashion stage, started up their own fashion houses, and became adults under the spotlight of the international fashion press, both artistically and as entrepreneurs.

This book and the exhibition it accompanies bear the title *Olivier Theyskens: She walks in beauty*, from a poem by Lord Byron written in 1813. This literary reference is not only a wink and a nod to the countless historical references in Olivier Theyskens' oeuvre and the atmosphere of dark romance in so many of his collections, but also a hint about the approach of the exhibition and the book. Both reveal how Theyskens' creative DNA has been in constant motion throughout the various stages of his career—as creative director for Rochas, Nina Ricci, and Theory—as he developed a consistent and mature signature. Motion is also characteristic of Theyskens' designs. He loves extraordinary fabrics, materials, and textile treatments, selected for the way they reflect light or fall around an active body. Combining that with meticulously developed tailoring, he generates a lightness that keeps his designs in motion and prevents them from becoming stranded in historic nostalgia. Indeed, Olivier Theyskens continually succeeds in presenting an image of fashion that is entirely his own and entirely up-to-date.

In the exhibition, this vision is superbly interpreted by Glenn Sestig Architects, who fully understand Theyskens' eye for material and motion. The firm has designed a setting that plays with the evolution of light to dark and all the subtle shadings in between. Curators Karen Van Godtsenhoven and Lydia Kamitsis convey the story of Theyskens' unique visual language with the aid of objects, drawings, and photography

It gives me great pleasure to thank both curators, Glenn Sestig, Bernard Tournemenne, and their team, as well as the designer of this publication, Philippe Galowich, photographer Julien Claessens, who has made new work for this book together with Thomas Deschamps, and the authors and photographers who have contributed to this volume. My thanks also to the entire MoMu team and the various (media) partners and sponsors who have helped bring this project to life. Finally, I extend my most heartfelt thanks to Olivier Theyskens and Agnès Magoga for their faith in MoMu. After fifteen years of producing exhibitions, and just before MoMu closes for two years of renovation and expansion, the presentation of Olivier Theyskens' first retrospective exhibition marks a very special moment.
We are happy that it will bring to a fitting close the first phase of the life of MoMu, even as we look forward to the future.

Kaat Debo

Director, MoMu—Fashion Museum Antwerp

Olivier Theyskens, Spring/Summer 1998, leather skirt, silk blouse with bead embroidery, and bodice with neckpiece in silk with vintage mourning jewelry.

All garments come from the Olivier Theyskens archives, except when stated otherwise.

Olivier Theyskens, Spring/Summer 1998, sleeveless coat in astrakhan, trousers in silk, and neckpiece in man-made fiber with embroidered vintage mourning jewelry.

Hymne à la beauté (extrait)
Charles Baudelaire

Viens-tu du ciel profond ou sors-tu de l'abîme
O Beauté ? Ton regard infernal et divin,
Verse confusément le bienfait et le crime,
Et l'on peut pour cela te comparer au vin.

Sors-tu du gouffre noir ou descends-tu des astres ?
Le destin charmé suit tes jupons comme un chien ;
Tu sèmes au hasard la joie et les désastres,
Et tu gouvernes tout et ne réponds de rien.

Olivier Theyskens, Spring/Summer 1998, dress in vintage lace, trimmed with vintage silk ruffles and flowers, and briefs in vintage lace.

left:
Olivier Theyskens, Spring/Summer 1998, dress in vintage lace with boned bodice in man-made toile.

right:
Olivier Theyskens, Fall/Winter 1998–99, dress in wool with high split and train, heart-shaped inset in lace, and vein motif embroidery. Python boots.

A une passante (extrait) Charles Baudelaire

La rue assourdissante autour de moi hurlait.
Longue, mince, en grand deuil, douleur majestueuse,
Une femme passa, d'une main fastueuse
Soulevant, balançant le feston et l'ourlet;

Olivier Theyskens, Fall/Winter 1998–99, tailored jacket with double lapel and hook-and-eye closure, skirt with train in cotton toile used for upholstery. Leather sandals.

Olivier Theyskens, Fall/Winter 1998–99, dress with high split in cotton toile used for upholstery, with hook-and-eye closure and train. Boots in cotton toile.

Olivier Theyskens, Fall/Winter 1998–99, leather cape, leather jacket with hook-and-eye closure, and leather skirt.

"(…) Dark, with brown hair, I don't recall. Young. Magnificent eyes that mingle languor with subtlety, cruelty, despair. Slender, dressed in dark colors, black silk stockings. And something *déclassé* about her that is sympathetic. (…)" p. 42

"Beauty will be CONVULSIVE or will not be at all." p. 160

Quotes André Breton: Nadja

Olivier Theyskens, Fall/Winter 1998–99, dress in cotton toile printed with a motif of Toile de Jouy with cords, bead embroidery, and tailored jacket in patent leather with boning.

Olivier Theyskens, Fall/Winter 1998–99, stole in vintage Chantilly lace and vintage quilted, checkered cotton. Leather sandals.

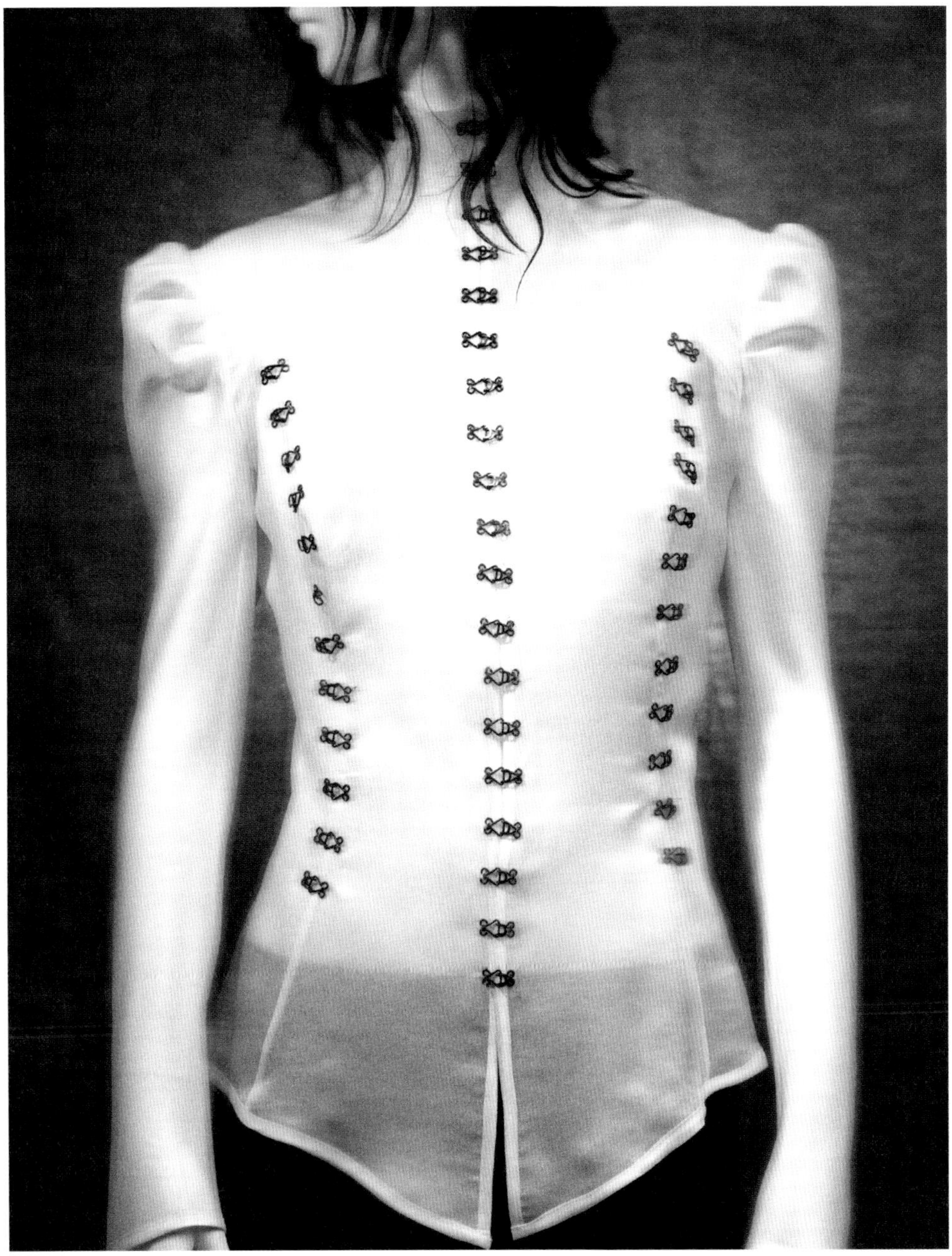

left:
Olivier Theyskens, Spring/Summer 1999, sleeveless, boned leather dress and trousers in wool.

right:
Olivier Theyskens, Spring/Summer 1999, blouse in man-made silk with hook-and-eye closure and applications on the back, and wool skirt.

Olivier Theyskens, Spring/Summer 1999,
strapless dress in silk, leather gloves with
hook-and-eye closure. Leather boots.

Olivier Theyskens, Spring/Summer 1999, blouse in silk and man-made fiber, skirt in silk, leather gloves with hook-and-eye closure. Leather boots.

Olivier Theyskens, Spring/Summer 1999, wool blazer with hair application on the back and wool trousers.

Olivier Theyskens, Spring/Summer 1999, dress in silk with hook-and-eye closure in the front in the shape of an open cross.

Olivier Theyskens, Fall/Winter 1999–00, leather cape with hood, double layered at the front with zipper and hook-and-eye closure, leather trousers with hook-and-eye closure on left leg and cross-shaped zippers on right leg. Leather boots.

Olivier Theyskens, Fall/Winter 1999–00, coat in squirrel fur with high split in the back and large hook-and-eye closure, leather trousers. Leather boots.

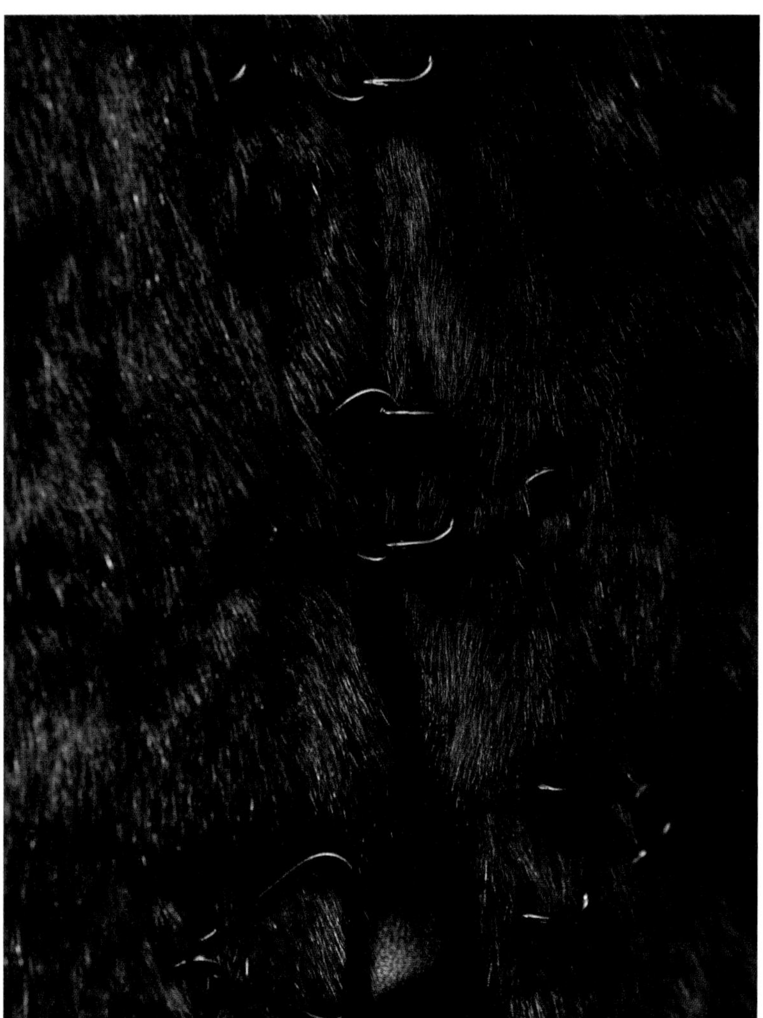

Olivier Theyskens, Fall/Winter 1999–00, blouse with asymmetrical collar in cotton with buttons and hook-and-eye closure, leather skirt with hook-and-eye closure on both sides. Leather shoes.

Olivier Theyskens, Fall/Winter 1999–00, raw silk dress with hook-and-eye closure on sleeves, linen boned bodice with hood and hook-and-eye closure.

Olivier Theyskens, Fall/Winter 1999–00, sleeveless leather coat with open sides and hook-and-eye closure, blazer in wool with hook-and-eye closure, and trousers in wool.

top left:

Olivier Theyskens, Spring/Summer 2000, leather bodice with lace and zipper closure in the back, skirt in coated silk. Leather boots.

top right:

Olivier Theyskens, Spring/Summer 2000, strapless dress in silk, underskirt in silk gauze. Leather shoes.

bottom left:

Olivier Theyskens, Spring/Summer 2000, sleeveless bias-cut silk dress with loose panels hanging from the back of the shoulders.

middle:

Olivier Theyskens, Spring/Summer 2000, leather bodysuit, leather skirt in the shape of a coat, and leather thong. Leather shoes.

lower right:

Olivier Theyskens, Spring/Summer 2000, coat with belt and strapless jumpsuit in cotton and linen. Leather boots.

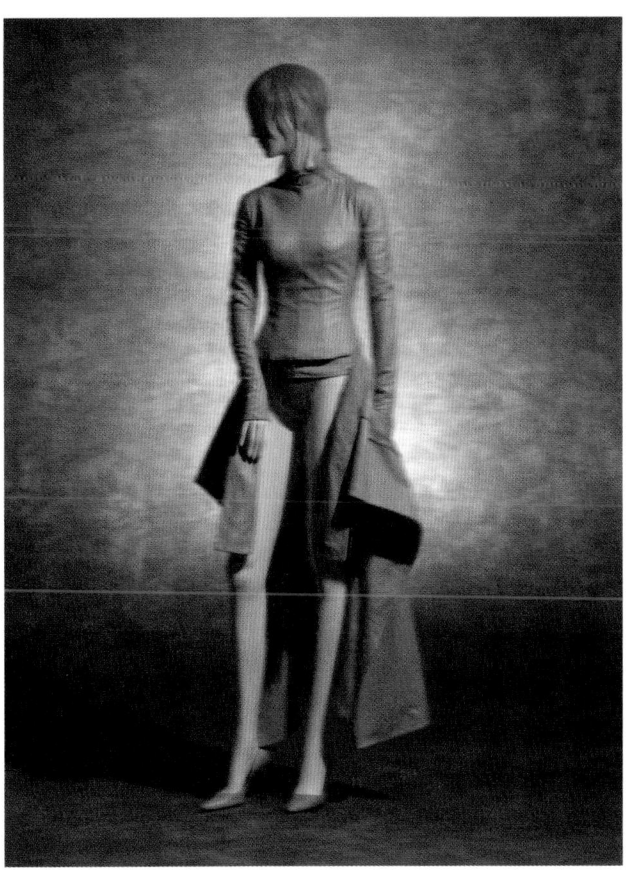

Olivier Theyskens, Spring/Summer 2000,
dress in coated linen with a long train.

left:
Olivier Theyskens, Fall/Winter 2000–01, bodice in lambskin with oversized, removable sleeves with zippers.

right:
Olivier Theyskens, Fall/Winter 2000–01, down jacket in lambskin with hood hidden in collar and oversized sleeves with zipper and button closures. Boots in lambskin.

Olivier Theyskens, Fall/Winter 2000–01,
jacket, dress, crinoline, shoes in silk moiré.

left:
Olivier Theyskens, Spring/Summer 2000, leather jumpsuit consisting of separate bodice and trousers zipped together, with hood hidden in collar. Leather pumps flocked with sand.

right:
Olivier Theyskens, Spring/Summer 2000, leather cape with hood hidden in collar and zipper.

left:
Olivier Theyskens, Spring/Summer 2001, sleeveless leather jacket with hood set into the collar, boned skirt in cotton with cords. Leather sandals flocked with sand.

right:
Olivier Theyskens, Spring/Sumer 2001, bias-cut silk dress, with belt in wool and cotton.

left:
Olivier Theyskens, Spring/Summer 2001, bias-cut dress in silk. Leather pumps flocked with sand.

right:
Olivier Theyskens, Spring/Summer 2001, bias-cut dress in silk.

Olivier Theyskens, Fall/Winter 2001–02, jacket in wool with attached, boned top with hook-and-eye closure and silk satin belt, strapless top in cotton, wrap skirt in wool and linen with lining in viscose worn inside out. Leather shoes.

Olivier Theyskens, Fall/Winter 2001–02, bra and underwear in silk satin, with scarf in silk voile.

Olivier Theyskens, Fall/Winter 2001–02,
dress in silk satin with pleated neckline,
decorated with rhinestones. Leather boots.

Olivier Theyskens, Spring/Summer 2002,
top in silk tulle trimmed in silk and linen, and
skirt in leather and cotton with sewn-in bustle.
Leather sandals.

Olivier Theyskens, Spring/Summer 2002, double-breasted trench coat and trousers in silk and man-made fiber. Leather shoes.

Olivier Theyskens, Spring/Summer 2002, dress in silk tulle with cotton ribbons partially structured with boning and underskirt in silk knit. Leather shoes.

Olivier Theyskens, Spring/Summer 2002, strapless top in the shape of a miniature jacket and skirt with sewn-in bustle in a mix of silk and man-made fiber. Leather sandals with stuffed canary.

Olivier Theyskens, Spring/Summer 2002, strapless top in the shape of a miniature jacket in linen, cotton, and silk with corset closure in the front. Skirt in cotton, linen, and silk with sewn-in bustle. Leather sandals with stuffed canary.

Rochas, Fall/Winter 2003–04, evening gown and jacket in printed silk, with bands of flounced lace on top, in imitation Chantilly bobbin lace. MoMu Collection T09/673AB

Rochas, Fall/Winter 2005–06, dress in silk crêpe. MoMu Collection B15/22

Rochas, Fall/Winter 2006–07, sleeveless dress in silk, viscose, and cotton with embroidery.

left:
Nina Ricci, Fall/Winter 2008–09, dress and multilayered skirt in silk with metal embroidery. Pumps in silk satin and leather. MoMu Collection B14/32, B14/33

right:
Nina Ricci, Spring/Summer 2009, dress in printed silk and knitted net with attached leggings. MoMu Collection B15/3

Nina Ricci, Spring/Summer 2009, double-breasted coat in bouclé weave in wool and man-made fiber with bead embroidery. Suede laced boots. MoMu Collection B15/3AB

Theyskens' Theory, Spring/Summer 2011,
blazer in wool.

Olivier Theyskens, Spring/Summer 2017, sleeveless dress and belt in checkered and plain viscose with long train with bead and sequin embroidery. MoMu Collection T17/850AB

Olivier Theyskens, Spring/Summer 2017, sleeveless dress in cotton with rubber coating, long train with bead embroidery and belt in leather and silk.

left:

Olivier Theyskens, Spring/Summer 2017, sleeveless dress with woven polka dots in organza. Leather boots with hook-and-eye closure.

middle:

Olivier Theyskens, Spring/Summer 2017, bias-cut dress in silk. Leather boots with hook-and-eye closure.

right:

Olivier Theyskens, Spring/Summer 2017, jacket and belt in python leather and multilayered skirt in silk and linen. Leather boots with hook-and-eye closure.

bottom left:

Olivier Theyskens, Spring/Summer 2017, dress in silk, with leather belt. Leather boots.

The Couture Spirit

Lydia Kamitsis
Independent Curator and Art Historian
Associate Curator for *She walks in beauty*

Olivier Theyskens, Spring/Summer 1998,
Moderne Magazine, Belgium, December 1997

While Olivier Theyskens' journey has spanned five sequential stages, each identified by its own distinctive brand, universe, aesthetic, position in the market, and unique characteristics, at least one principle has been a constant throughout his body of work: the principle of poetic spirit. Poetic in the sense of being capable of expressing beauty, based on the word's ancient Greek etymology, the verb ποιεῖν (poiein), meaning to make or to create. Theyskens personifies both the metaphorical and literal definitions of poetic spirit.

That poetic spirit might also be deemed "couture spirit," a more conventional expression that Theyskens himself has used many times. No matter which way you word it, this spirit captures the designer's approach to his profession, his work ethos, and the way he channels his vision through his collections—it is not merely about the professional field in which he operates.[1]

Indistinguishable from the Theyskens brand, this spirit manifested itself early on, during his childhood. In his family home, there is a workshop, a sewing room. There, Olivier watches his mother closely, fascinated by the process of sewing and trying in vain to decode the sequence of operations she performs on the machine. His sense of creativity grows even stronger when, at his grandparents' house in Normandy, he discovers a magical treasure trove: dozens of carefully labeled boxes containing various items of haberdashery, collected and saved for future use. There are boxes filled with buttons, hooks, fasteners, ribbons, scraps of fur, lace, spools of different types of thread—all the entries that in the future will fill the couturier's own thesaurus.

First aesthetic emotions and first feelings of wonder: the pleasure of handling fabrics that drape in various ways. He possesses a curiosity about textiles from an early age, alongside his childhood propensity for dressing up. Dreaming of the majestic life of a princess with a long cape draped over her shoulders, he attaches cushions to his belt to create an archaic crinoline.

This passion for clothing remains unchanged throughout his adolescence, and the prestigious La Cambre fashion school becomes the obvious next step for an eighteen-year-old obsessed with sketching. But his impatience and dissatisfaction with the program lead him to abandon his studies after two years.

As a result of his abridged academic education, Theyskens is not exposed to the basic rules and practices of the industry, but rather than holding him back in his evolution as a designer, this shortened study period gives Theyskens a sense of freedom that will serve him well. Having never had to follow the example of others or use a specific methodology developed by his elders, he enters the world of fashion as a neophyte, filled with fresh ideas and the naïve dreams of a self-taught designer.

He proceeds without a pre-established model other than the notion that a beautiful garment should be well cut. To achieve this, he will surmount his own lack of knowledge by means of lucid determination, insatiable curiosity, and round-the-clock work.

He singlehandedly makes all the patterns for his first two collections, sewing most of the pieces himself in Brussels with the enthusiastic help of a few close friends. During these formative years, Theyskens' attention to detail grows even stronger and he establishes rigorous production requirements. Sewn by hand and crafted from reclaimed materials, such as lace, linen dishtowels, and artisanal embroideries, these prototypes are then impossible to produce in a factory. And despite the risk of alienating buyers put off by a beginner's unorthodox attitude, Theyskens decides he will not commercialize any collection until a satisfactory production system is established.

The couture spirit lives in this absolute quest for perfection.

George Rodenbach – Le règne du silence (1891): Au fil de l'âme

VI

Les rêves sont les clés pour sortir de nous-même,
(...)
Une vie extatique où ne cheminent plus
Que des rêves, vêtus de mousseline blanche...

For his third collection, working to address the challenge of making a bias cut skirt, Theyskens hires a pattern maker and is stunned to see her work directly on the material without any calculations or preliminary steps. It is a moment of revelation! He realizes now that a designer can proceed directly to this stage, once he has thought through and mentally visualized a clear and precise idea of a garment's volume—something Theyskens has already mastered. His sketches, like blueprints for his creations, include every minute detail of the garments he envisions.

Gifted with both a mathematical and an artistic mindset, Theyskens masters the technique of cutting and understands the fine points of pattern making; he enjoys sewing and endlessly exploring the many possible equations that exist between volume, fabrics of different textures and weights, and the body that will make it all come to life. His exhaustive research encompasses every detail of a garment, from the selection of different types of fasteners to the invisible finishing, the lining, and the many accessories; each element is given an equal amount of attention and importance.

Having acquired his expertise empirically, Theyskens develops a real give-and-take with the workshops involved in the production process. They are close collaborators, and the designer will maintain an ongoing, almost family-like relationship with small Italian production units for more than fifteen years.

The couture spirit lives in this method of examining every detail, in a quasi-artisanal manner, with a fluid exchange between like-minded craftsmen who speak the same technical language.

That spirit also lives in the appreciation of handcraftsmanship and in the stylish attitude that welcomes a challenge while avoiding the most obvious ways of using numerous technical skills and established innovations.

This couture spirit, which serves as both a method and a goal, runs through Theyskens' oeuvre and reaches its peak when he accepts the challenge to revive the house of Rochas, a "sleeping beauty" ripe for rebirth at the start of the twenty-first century. The timing is, in fact, perfect: the post-war world of haute couture—represented by Marcel Rochas providing an image of femininity on the verge of a profound aesthetic upheaval—merges with the designer's very personal vision. It is as if Theyskens has prepared for this exceptional moment all along.

In the essay "The Painter of Modern Life," published in 1863, Charles Baudelaire outlines the characteristics of genius in these words: "But genius is no more than childhood recaptured at will, childhood equipped now with man's physical means to express itself, and with the analytical mind that enables it to bring order into the sum of experience, involuntarily amassed. To this deep and joyful curiosity must be attributed that stare, animal-like in its ecstasy, which all children have when confronted with something new, whatever it may be, face or landscape, light, gilding, colors, watered silk, enchantment of beauty, enhanced by the arts of dress."

A century and a half later, Baudelaire's definition perfectly suits Theyskens. I ask the designer about the spirit that drives him: "What excites me," he answers, "is the process of discovery, entering unknown territory, like the first time I made a pair of trousers, a shirt, a tailored jacket. It's the technical exploration that fuels me."

In the September 28, 2015 edition of *Le Monde*, he is quoted as saying, "It's true, I have created many different things but what I care most about is precision and well thought-out beauty. I am motivated by what is accessible, as I am by the idea that what is inaccessible is a dream. I can devote as much time to a T-shirt as I will to a shapely and very fluid evening gown."

That says it all.

1 Nor should the term "couture" be confused with the phrase "haute couture," a designation that is legally protected and is granted in France by the Chambre Syndicale de la Haute Couture to a limited number of fashion houses that meet very specific criteria.

left:
Olivier Theyskens, Spring/Summer 1998,
Moderne Magazine, Belgium, December 1997

right:
Olivier Theyskens, Spring/Summer 1998,
"Madonna Chooses Dare" *Spin Magazine*, April 1998

left:
Olivier Theyskens, Spring/Summer 1998,
Moderne Magazine, Belgium, December 1997

right:
Olivier Theyskens, Spring/Summer 1998,
W magazine, June 1998

All tomorrow's parties —— 1966
The Velvet Underground

And what costume shall the poor girl wear
To all tomorrow's parties
A hand-me-down dress from who knows where
To all tomorrow's parties
And where will she go, and what shall she do
When midnight comes around
A blackened shroud
A hand-me-down gown
Of rags and silks, a costume
Fit for one who sits and cries
For all tomorrow's parties

Olivier Theyskens, Spring/Summer 1998,
Catalogue

On Corsets and the Body

Lydia Kamitsis
Independent Curator and Art Historian
Associate Curator for *She walks in beauty*

A disquieting and paradoxical accessory, the corset is an essential element of Olivier Theyskens' stylistic code and an integral feature of the Gothic romantic universe regularly featured in the media.

One of Theyskens' earliest creations, a black corset worn by Madonna in January 1998 at the Sanremo festival, would propel the young prodigy into the spotlight. And when the pop star attended the VH1 awards in October of that year wearing a corseted gown embellished with hooks and eyes—another distinctive element of the Theyskens style—the world took notice, effectively launching the designer's career.

Since then, a form of the corset has appeared in every collection of his, whether incorporated into a gauzy dress of black lace or transformed into an exquisite collar embroidered with jets to add a regal look to the face. It can take the shape of a rigid cocoon that protectively envelops both the torso and the head, or take on the form of a modern-day corset, a *guêpière*—an homage to its inventor, Marcel Rochas, the designer whose brand's revival was entrusted to Theyskens.

Worn directly against the skin or over a dress, as an integral part of the structure of a garment or as a completely independent piece, as a more or less discreet undergarment or a bold and visible accessory, the corset is the nerve center of the Theyskens silhouette.

Serving as the leitmotif in his work, the corset is rarely a random feature—never a manifestation of a fad or a passing interest in a bygone period. Instead, it is the cornerstone of the designer's concept of ideal beauty, the foundation on which his childhood emotions developed into deep aesthetic aspirations. It is a fundamental, archaic piece—in the etymological sense of the word, ἀρχή, *arché*, the origin…

Emblematic of a long history of acquiescence to the dogma of a tiny waist and a body constrained to achieve a certain posture, the whalebone corset would become incompatible with women's emancipation during the 1920s and was virtually banished in modern times. Still, it never truly disappeared from the world of fantasy. With its strong erotic connotation, the corset lived on in the fringes of fetishism until it began making sporadic appearances on the runways.

During the 1980s, a period that embraced eclectic references with a penchant for recycling the shapes and customs of the past, designers naturally turned their attention to the corset. They no longer used it as an undergarment but instead treated it as a garment unto itself, infused with new contradictory messages.

Seen as an art object due to both its technical and symbolic complexity, the corset can evoke sexuality or violence, as well as convention or nostalgia, as designers explore its multiple forms and meanings and develop even newer interpretations. In the wake of his illustrious predecessors, Theyskens approaches the subject in his way, through the lens of his own artistic concerns and experiences.

If a cherished grandmother's girdle is the catalyst for Jean Paul Gaultier's "signature" corset, shown in infinite variations throughout his collections, engravings from the nineteenth century triggered Olivier Theyskens' childhood fantasies. Images of Victorian gowns, whose volume seemed all the more extraordinary when compared to the tiny waists that supported them, sparked the designer's imagination. He was struck by their look of fragility and grandeur.

"As a child, I thought a full crinoline was the epitome of beauty," recalls Theyskens. "Creating a beautiful and perfectly proportioned crinoline was the way to attain absolute grace and beauty on the scale of a fashion engraving." To achieve such fascinating fullness, which was an abstract composition of sorts, the designer intuitively feels the need for a corset that serves as a structural foundation or a necessary anchor.

Rochas, Spring/Summer 2005, *The New York Times Style Magazine*, October 2004

Olivier Theyskens, Fall/Winter 1999–00,
Visionaire, 1999

There are other couturiers known for their corseted silhouettes, among them Vivienne Westwood, Christian Lacroix, and John Galliano, who are also recognized for their knowledge of the subject. But historical reference was never Olivier Theyskens' goal, probably because he preferred to revisit the fleeting impressions locked away in his memory—impressions that immediately merged with his own ideal of beauty—rather than allude to the beautiful shapes of the past.

Fantasy is more inspiring than reality, and one can appreciate the shock that must have been experienced by this dreamer when his vision of splendid gowns with huge trains "in the style of James Tissot" came up against the reality of the bustle dresses Theyskens saw at a historical costume exhibition. This was a different reality, much more restrained, with ordinary proportions—a reality that shattered his dreams.

His fantasy initially thwarted, the designer would eventually channel his disappointment by creating astonishing bustle evening gowns for the summer of 2002. Molded to the body and perfectly executed, though with smaller proportions, the dresses exuded an unusual melancholic beauty.

"My desire is above all to make girls beautiful. To make them sexy is not my aim," declares the designer, explaining his idiosyncratic approach. When designing corsets, Theyskens captures their power of seduction yet avoids any exaggerated girly references.

The border between beautiful and sexy is even more marked in the high-risk challenge Theyskens undertook in reviving the house of Rochas.

A softer avatar of the whalebone corset, the *guêpière* was invented by Marcel Rochas during the war: by calling attention to the waistline, it played a major role in the hypersexuality of the new feminine silhouette imposed by Dior's New Look, a style that emphasized precisely molded and controlled curves. Theyskens transformed this emblematic piece into a lighter weight bodice, free of stays, a design that is constantly being improved and whose production is overseen by the house's ateliers, allowing them to keep a close eye on this particular display of expertise.

In an ultimate step toward modernization, the most recent version of the *guêpière* shows off the full measure of the Theyskens method. Deconstructed into two separate pieces (a bra and a corset) held together by a few stitches, it easily adjusts to any length torso. This new guêpière meets a woman's needs and lifestyle, respects her individuality, and proves that the desire for comfort is not inconsistent with the pursuit of beauty.

The Sensuality and Refinement of Lace

Wim Mertens
Curator, MoMu

Olivier Theyskens gives femininity a personal interpretation based on a sensibility that he exhibited at an early age. In his hands, sensuality and natural grace are translated through close attention to materials and craftsmanship. In many of his collections, lace makes a major contribution to this image of femininity.

Throughout history, lace has served as a bridge between the body and the outside world. Theyskens incorporated black lace into his earliest designs.[1] Worn directly against the skin, the lace offered transparency that created erotic tension. That tension in turn helped express his fetishism for the beauty of the naked body. The link to lingerie is both subtle and explicit.

Lace was first produced in the first half of the sixteenth century and initially was used for border decoration and insets in linens. Ultimately, around 1600, lace also began to appear as decoration on upper body clothing for both women and men. Bands of lace, including black lace, were appliquéd to clothing in geometric patterns. By the end of the seventeenth century, lace was covering whole sections of upper body apparel. For this, open lace with floral and vine motifs was used, and the motifs were connected to one another with bars or transparent backgrounds. Often applied to light-colored silk fabrics, the dark lace stood out handsomely. (Sadly, very little seventeenth-century black lace has survived. The silk fiber was damaged by aggressive components inherent to the process of dyeing it black.[2]) At the time, black lace was produced in Italy, France, and the Southern Netherlands, with Genoa, Paris, Lille, and Antwerp major centers of trade and production.[3]

Up to the first half of the seventeenth century, black lace was also used in men's fashions, but its use in men's clothing then fell out of favor. By the turn of the eighteenth century, black lace was, in any case, losing its popularity. In 1750, however, it was thoroughly restored to fashion in the form of capes, shawls, and coiffure elements that featured thin floral motifs on a fine mesh background. Segments of these were made of expensive silk Chantilly lace.[4] During those years, black lace was an entirely feminine phenomenon in terms of both the clothing to which it was applied and its appearance.

Chantilly lace continued to be greatly loved in the nineteenth century, and its popularity grew further after about 1830. It was characterized by large, often naturalistic floral motifs. Notably spectacular were large shawls and wide lace bands on full skirts made of this type of lace. Production took place in the French cities of Bayeux and Caen, and later also in Geraardsbergen in Belgium.

In the 1840s, it became possible to produce imitations of Chantilly bobbin lace by machine.[5] Machine-made lace was not necessarily seen as inferior. On the contrary, it was a product of industrial progress and was loved precisely because of that, even by royalty and the well-to-do bourgeoisie. For the first time, lace in large sizes was available to the middle classes. In the twentieth century, big couture houses and lingerie manufacturers began to purchase considerable amounts of machine-made lace, which was often embroidered or finished by hand.

Olivier Theyskens, Spring/Summer 1998,
Moderne Magazine, Belgium, December 1997

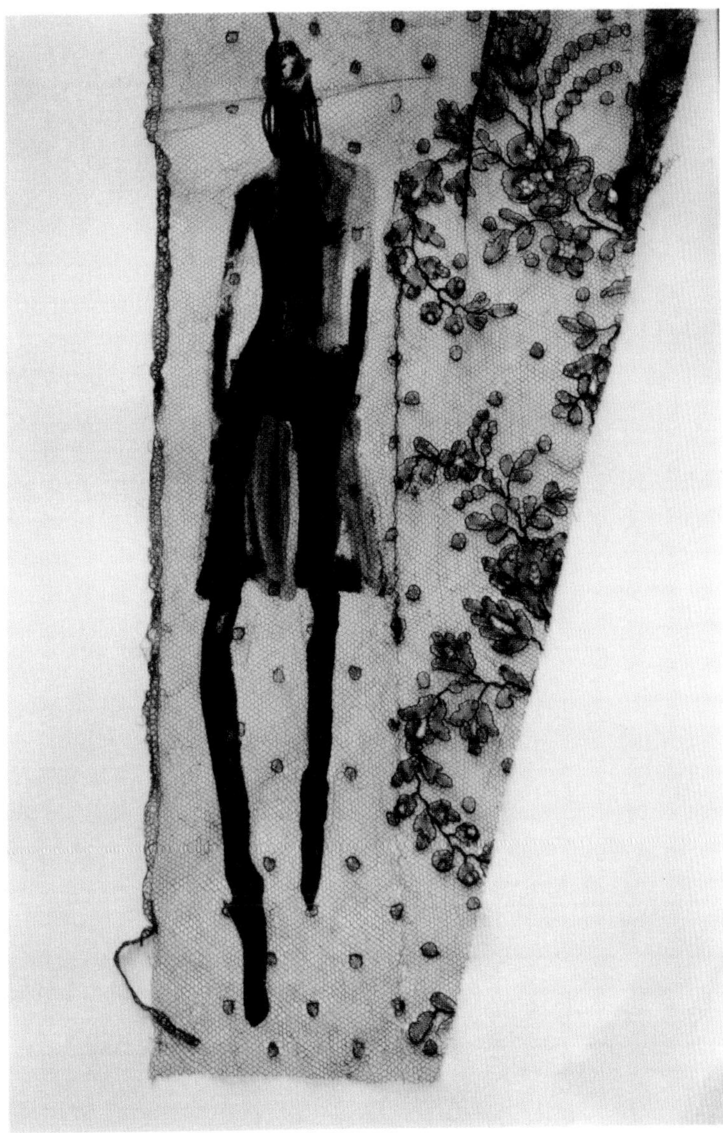

Rochas, Fall/Winter 2003–04,
Vogue Italia, July 2003

Black Chantilly lace was the trademark of the Rochas house from the time it introduced its Femme perfume in 1944. Lace again appeared in the house's signature evening dress in 1946 and the iconic 1948 *guêpière* corset, with its black Chantilly lace combined with soft pink satin. In his silhouettes for Rochas, Olivier Theyskens built upon the affinity Marcel Rochas felt for Chantilly lace to evoke a sensual, sophisticated femininity.[6] In doing so, he echoed the age-old tradition of using lace for both outer apparel and undergarments and pairing it with silk fabrics in matching or contrasting colors. Theyskens used lace in large, wide-lobed bands on flouncing for skirts and sleeves and on groundwork of black and pink silk. Materials and colors, volumes, and cut all reflected the DNA of the house. Chantilly lace motifs were also used in prints on silk fabrics. Rochas Chantilly lace was produced by Sophie Hallette, a firm in Caudry in northern France, which has a long history in couture dating back to 1887. Marcel Rochas was a customer as well.

In his designs for Rochas, Theyskens revealed the refined character of lace and its connection to French haute couture, as well as its association with an adult, self-aware femininity. This is in contrast to the sometimes open, risqué, and erotic character of the designer's early work, which expressed a girlish, in-the-bud femininity.

1 Lynn Hirschberg, "Is There a Place for Olivier Theyskens?" *The New York Times Magazine*, August 6, 2006.
2 Seventeenth-century black lace has survived as samples in archives and on rare pieces of contemporary clothing. The city archives of Antwerp and the Plantin-Moretus archives have trade documents that include samples of black lace. Clothing with black lace is preserved in the Hessisches Landesmuseum in Darmstadt, the Germanisches Nationalmuseum in Nuremberg, and the Royal Armoury in Stockholm. These are all samples of bobbin lace.
3 Marguerite Coppens, "The Trade and Production of Lace in the Southern Netherlands During the Seventeenth Century: New Data, in Particular on the Subject of Black Lace," *Riggisberger Berichte* 19 (2012): 71–79.
4 Chantilly lace is named after the village of the same name, to the northwest of Paris, and began to be produced there in the late seventeenth century. Production stopped during the French Revolution. Chantilly lace was produced in bobbin sections that afterward were joined together to form larger pieces.
5 Pat Earnshaw, *The Identification of Lace* (Aylesbury: Shire Publications, 1980), 128–129.
6 L Hirschberg, Ibidem.

40

On Movement

Lydia Kamitsis
Independent Curator and Art Historian
Associate Curator for *She walks in beauty*

Olivier Theyskens' designs are often paradoxical: the corset, a garment that implies static posture, appears throughout a body of work largely based on movement and the exploration of clothing's dynamic quality.

Indeed, one need only look at any of his collections, regardless of the label (Olivier Theyskens, Rochas, Nina Ricci, Theory), to see that each concerns a woman in motion, usually with her hands in her pockets, often seen in profile, sometimes from the back. This underscores the importance of movement in the designer's vision of ideal style. The choreography of a woman in motion—undulating, oscillating, gliding, floating, or maintaining her balance—is achieved through Theyskens' meticulous attention to the details of every design.

Selection of fabrics and accessories, as well as the tiniest hook-and-eye closures, the technique of cut and assembly, arrangement of all the different elements that make up the look, particular attention lavished on the back of the garment: every detail is carefully studied so that they combine to create a certain allure. This method is geared to anticipating the way a garment will react when the woman wearing it is in motion.

Whether a garment increases or constrains movement, its structure exudes a specific energy that imparts a feeling of freedom or power and affects a woman's sense of self. For this purpose, Theyskens has always sought out the most intriguing materials, those with innate characteristics that lead to new and innovative applications.

Each fabric is carefully selected according to its weight, texture, and ability to allow movement. Thin, fine, and slightly transparent textiles such as chiffon and tulle will flow differently as they catch the air, depending on their density. Other, more fluid fabrics fall more or less rapidly in an almost liquid fashion. Thus they create folds that can vary in fullness. Firmer fabrics, such as taffeta, interact with the light, resulting in a shimmering effect.

Each fabric requires a specific technique, a particular method of cutting to achieve the desired result. The effects of fluidity and sensuality, combined with the *flou* technique, give Theyskens' creations a kind of sobriety and gentle restraint. The soft line of his full double-breasted jackets from the Spring/Summer 1999 collection is achieved through an asymmetric closure; avoiding the rigid fall of a masculine cut the trousers from the Fall/Winter 2008-09 Nina Ricci collection seem to undulate. The dresses, skirts, and expertly crafted coats of the Fall/Winter 2001-02 collection convey a sense of fluidity thanks to the double layering of fabric that allows air to circulate.

Understanding the mechanics of the bias cut is a challenge for any designer. Organic in nature with an inherent sense of movement, it takes time to master this cut. Theyskens relishes the challenge and endlessly tests its limits. For instance, by placing his hands on a garment in progress, he can evaluate its potential for rotation as he embraces its magical complexity.

His first collection for Nina Ricci, Fall/Winter 2007-08, was fueled by the spiral and directly inspired by L'Air du Temps, the brand's emblematic fragrance. This gave Theyskens an opportunity to explore plasticity while following in the steps of Madeleine Vionnet, the ultimate master of the bias.

Examining the concept of the garment in motion, by all possible means, is the subject of another exceptional collection for Nina Ricci, the Spring/Summer 2009 collection.

Inspired by the world of dance, Theyskens imagines dresses that are short in the front and longer in the back, each with its own way of moving. From floating trains that skim over padded derrières to skirts that flow at each step to reveal the legs, the designer exhibits his mastery at choosing the size and placement of every flounce, as well as understanding the specific texture of the chiffon, satin, or tulle that would create the full effect of the animated silhouette he had envisaged.

Additional measures can be taken to provoke a particular movement of the body. For the Fall/Winter 2009-10 Nina Ricci collection, shoes are extravagant in terms of both style and height, causing the models to walk with extra care, adding a sense of weightlessness. As a consequence of their voluminous structure, and depending on their weight, crinoline skirts, a leitmotif of Theyskens' collections, glide majestically or merrily swing back and forth as models walk the runway.

Theyskens' interest in movement and the garments' dynamic power is evident in the way the designer studies a single silhouette from different perspectives, specifically in his approach to the profile and the back of each piece.

As a child, Theyskens was fascinated by peacocks, magnificent birds whose tails resemble beautiful trains. The image of the peacock is eloquently revisited in Theyskens' designs for the backs of his creations. The backs of his dresses are remarkable. They are embellished with pleats, folds, unexpected embroidery, openwork motifs held together with hooks and eyes, daring décolletages, but also floating panels, bows hidden under layers of lace, trains—an entire world of surprises reminiscent of the nineteenth-century engravings that were so appealing to the designer when he was young. In those etchings, crinolines and bustle dresses were usually depicted from the side or from a three-quarter perspective highlighting the more elaborate parts of the dress in contrast to the fronts, which were usually simple and free of ornamentation.

The side profile of a silhouette indubitably possesses a certain elegance and photogenic flair. This approach was successfully employed in Theyskens' first Rochas collection, which was drawn completely in profile. Featuring rounded backs with exaggerated and voluminous curves and wide layered flounces that cut an almost abstract and disjointed figure, Theyskens' work for that collection sought to instill a new aesthetic of stylized motion, a certain hieratic sobriety in line with what was at stake.

Movement, as conceptualized by Theyskens, is never accidental or the natural consequence of fabric draped on a body in motion. Rather, it is intentional, the result of a complex study that defines his vision of a strong, free, confident woman, a woman of her time who, with a graceful, dancing, and light-footed step, always walks in beauty.

"Je ne m'intéresse pas à la façon dont les gens bougent, mais à ce qui les meut et à ce qu'ils font bouger". Pina Bausch

Black in the Oeuvre of Olivier Theyskens

A Complex Web of Associations

Wim Mertens
Curator, MoMu

Olivier Theyskens, Spring/Summer 1998

Because it has so many diverse and even diametrically opposed meanings, the color black has a complex history in the context of European fashion. It has always existed, yet its popularity has fluctuated over the years. Over time, wearing black has sent various signals about the social circles in which one moves and about specific events, such as weddings or periods of mourning. It has even sent messages about one's allegiance to a given region or a certain ruler.

Although black has been associated with specific social groups, such as the clergy and the magistrature, as far as we know, no one has ever been denied permission to wear it, not even under the sumptuary laws to control consumption that have been instated at various times since the Middle Ages. For mourning, black has been a constant. Among its earliest connotations were sadness and piety.[1] For fashionable apparel, black has always had an ongoing association with wealth and refinement. Now and then, black has become widely fashionable during an official period of mourning. For many years, deep black fabric, whether wool or silk, was expensive.[2] As a result, deep-black mourning-wear and fashionable clothing were accessible only to the wealthiest people, so the color became inextricably linked to court royalty and the structures of power.

It was only with the rise of industrial applications of aniline dyeing in the latter half of the nineteenth century that black became more affordable, and as a result it became more democratically distributed. Textile manufacturers promoted black fabrics in department stores, where they were greedily purchased by the middle classes and used to make both fashionable items and mourning-wear.[3] For the first time, these articles now were within reach of large groups of society.[4]

In the twentieth century, little changed in the old connotations and meanings associated with black. Black became an accepted color for formal clothing, was seen as distinguished and elegant, and was still worn as a sign of mourning. Eventually, the great interest in and availability of fashionable black textiles led to the birth of the iconic little black dress, the paragon of modernity, functionality, and elegance, and, according to Christian Dior, "a must in every woman's wardrobe."[5]

Finally, the association of black clothing with rebellion grew out of a succession of intellectual movements and subcultures in the post-World War II West, with the spread of the punk movement and Goth culture (characterized by a preference for black, fetishism, and a historic style of dress) supplying more recent devotees of black.[6]

In Olivier Theyskens' earliest collections, models wore heavy black makeup and were clothed in black silhouettes that were reminiscent of the Gothic style.[7] This led the fashion press to label the designer the "Prince of Darkness," "fashion's king of Goth," and a couturier who saw the world as a "dark Gothic place."[8] Indeed, the tailoring and the use of black fabrics do evoke associations with subcultures and with historic and contemporary tendencies in fashion. But black was first and foremost an inherent part of his design process. It helped him in his search for forms and silhouettes.[9] For Theyskens, therefore, the choice of black is partly functional. In addition, he has explained in interviews how his creations flow from an intermingling of impressions, reminiscences, cultures, and feelings from the present and the past.[10] The use of black can be seen as a part of his creative process, as diverse layers of meaning of the color black, both historical and contemporary, cross over and enrich one another.

In Theyskens' early work, black was an externalization of a dark, melancholy mood. He said it evoked what he defined as "sad happiness" and indicated that there were all kinds of concepts it could bring to bear: sadomasochism, severity, classic chic, mourning, and so on.[11] At the time, the designer sought a very deep black, one that could best be achieved in woolen fabrics. This meant that the association with mourning was quickly established.

In the past, in contrast to matte, muted black or ash gray mourning apparel, which was generally made of wool, fashionable black clothing was often made of expensive, shiny weaves that were richly decorated according to the current fashion and worn with accessories deemed to exude status, luxury, and elegance.

In Theyskens' work for the house of Rochas, with its history of French couture and glossy silk fabrics, the association with black was predominantly one of elegance and luxury that evolved from the long tradition of fashionable black clothing in European court cultures.

Black is a complex amalgam of historic and contemporary associations and meanings. In the case of Olivier Theyskens, one must not equate the color with a single spectrum. It is functional, and it refers to mourning and melancholy, but also to refinement and costliness. Ultimately, it constitutes an inherent part of his unique style, emanating from a complex creative process.

1 Lou Taylor, "Zwart als rouwkleur," in *Zwart. Meesterlijk zwart in mode & kostuum* [Black: masters of black in fashion and costume], ed. Kaat Debo, Wim Mertens, and Karen Van Godtsenhoven (Antwerp: MoMu, 2010), 129-139; and Bianca du Mortier, "De zwarte dood en andere rouwverhalen," in ibid., 144–153.
2 Natalia Ortega Saez, "De technologie van het zwartverven," in *Zwart*, 56–65.
3 Wim Mertens and Karen Van Godtsenhoven, "Zwart in de Europese mode," in *Manières noires. Zwart in beeldende kunsten, mode, design en elders*, ed. Alice Cantigniau (Mons: BAM Mons, 2010), 122.
4 Lou Taylor, "Zwart als rouwkleur," in *Zwart*, 128–139
5 Emmanuelle Dirix, "*La petite robe noire. De status van zwart in de mode van de jaren 1920,*" in *Zwart*, 163-179. Birgit Haase, [The little black dress: the Chanel 'Ford], in *Mythos Chanel* [The Chanel legend], ed. Maria Spitz (Mettingen: Draiflessen Collection, 2013), 182–191.
6 Mertens and Van Godtsenhoven, 127-128.
7 see K. Debo, "Meesterlijk zwart in mode en kostuum," in *Zwart*, 2010, p. 35.
8 Respectively, Lucy Ryder Richardson, "Prince of Darkness," *i-D*, July 1999; Lynn Hirschberg, "Is There a Place for Olivier Theyskens?" *The New York Times Magazine*, August 6, 2006; Constance White, "Galliano's Dance for Dior," *The New York Times*, October 14, 1998.
9 Kaat Debo, Idem, p. 42.
10 Dorian Grinspan, "Olivier Theyskens Speaks to Dorian Grinspan, Founder of *Out of Order* Magazine," *The Business of Fashion*, May 22, 2013, https://www.businessoffashion.com/articles/bof-exclusive/bof-exclusive-olivier-theyskens-speaks-to-dorian-grinspun-young-founder-of-out-of-order-magazine; Donatien Grau, "Olivier Theyskens," *AnOther Magazine*, May 21, 2012, http://www.anothermag.com/fashion-beauty/1962/olivier-theyskens.
11 Kaat Debo, Ibidem.

previous spread:
Rochas, Fall/Winter 2003–04

Olivier Theyskens, Spring/Summer 1999,
Elle France, March 1999

Sylvia Plath, Poppies in October, 1962
Even the sun-clouds this morning cannot manage such skirts.

Eros & Thanatos

Karen Van Godtsenhoven
Exhibition Curator, MoMu

Olivier Theyskens, Spring/Summer 1998,
Catalogue

Since the romantic poet Giacomo Leopardi's dialogue between Death and her sister, Fashion, the two concepts have been linked, thanks to their compelling and destructive natures. Fashion, as a succession of death and rebirth, binds Eros and Thanatos, two driving forces that play a major role in Sigmund Freud's psychoanalysis. As a playing field for erotic and morbid powers, fashion functions as society's subconscious. Obsessions, fears, and unfulfilled fantasies are acted out by the eye, the body, and fabrics: it is this interaction that we find in Olivier Theyskens' work. Freud claimed that fetishism primarily played out through leather, velvet, and fur, because these are lifeless materials in close proximity to naked body parts. Julia Kristeva, in turn, defined the abject as something that distinguishes itself from the subject and yet is not an object, such as the intestines, the skeleton, and excretions—all parts of our bodies that disgust us and pose a threat to the symbolic order. Freud's concept of the uncanny, something that seems both strange and familiar, is different from the abject in the sense that it does not constitute a part of ourselves. The use of leather and fur (for example astrakhan, the curly fleece of the unborn lamb), the embroidered wig on the back of a jacket in Theyskens' Spring/Summer 1999 collection, and the bodysuit embroidered with veins from Fall/Winter 1998-99 reveal his fascination for the fetish, the uncanny, and the abject.

Psychoanalysis claims that clothing, intertwined for as long as we can remember with rituals, magic, and worship, is full of references, as well as revenants: the fashion designer activates subconscious images from the past, which come to the surface in fashion. Such archetypes as the femme fatale, the female vampire, Lolita, and the madwoman locked in the attic are all expressions of the link between female sexuality, danger, and trauma.

The stated theme of Olivier Theyskens' first collection was "a perverse young girl living in a castle who braves the forbidden." She is a transgressive character who raids her surroundings to drape herself in old linens and other textiles. She is Theyskens' take on one of Charles Baudelaire's modern heroines, the *chiffonnier*, or ragpicker, a typical figure from nineteenth-century Paris. Another echo in this early work refers more to the end of the nineteenth century, to illness and trauma, a fascination that was characteristic of fashion designers in the late 1990s. The style was called "heroin chic." This sickly style reminds one of the women addicted to morphine in the Belle Époque in Paris. These women, often prostitutes, connected fin-de-siècle anxiety with female sexuality: beauty and angst united in a single image. Indeed, the prostitute was another of Baudelaire's modern heroines.

Young adolescent girls populate several of Theyskens' collections. In his work for Nina Ricci and Rochas, we see archetypes of innocence, including implicit desire and a Proustian dormant or smoldering sexuality, expressed with ostrich feathers, ruching, and chiffon. The intermingling of innocence and nostalgia makes one think of the romantic Miss Havisham in *Great Expectations*: the young girl caught in time as she grows old, living in a decrepit mansion and always wearing her wedding dress, after being abandoned at the altar. For Theyskens, these are two sides of the same coin, a symbol of the incomplete in female sexuality. There are no mature femmes fatales, no matriarchs here.

Miss Havisham brings us to another archetype, that of the madwoman in the attic, a cliché from nineteenth-century literature, in which women are often depicted as either innocent or monstrous. Theyskens celebrates divergent, even deviant expressions of female sexuality. In the edition of *A Magazine #D* that he guest-curated, he honored Swiss outsider artist Aloïse Corbaz (who began creating work in the 1920s), who populated her creations with medieval princesses and historic figures made of found or discarded materials. These included the sap from flower petals, pounded leaves, and toothpaste. Her naïve, *brut* drawings were populated with innocent heroines, often with bared breasts. Likewise, in his Spring/Summer 2004 collection for Rochas, Theyskens mixed naïve natural motifs with relatively demure reveals and décolletés made of black lace.

André Breton, editor of the surrealist magazine *Minotaure*, wrote about three kinds of convulsive, or all-encompassing beauty: the *explosante-fixe* (static, yet bursting with energy), the *magique-circonstancielle* (magical due to circumstances), and the *érotique-voilée* (veiled eroticism). Theyskens' fragile balance between Eros and Thanatos—his *érotique-voilée*—possesses the same melancholy beauty that Baudelaire discovered in the veiled widow in *A une passante*.

Select Bibliography
Bancroft, Alison. *Fashion and Psychoanalysis: Styling the Self.* London: Tauris, 2012.
Baudelaire, Charles. *Les fleurs du mal* [*The Flowers of Evil*]. Oxford: Oxford University Press, 1998.
Evans, Caroline. *Fashion at the Edge: Spectacle, Modernity, and Deathliness.* New Haven: Yale University Press, 2003.
Goffman, Erving. *The Presentation of Self in Everyday Life.* London: Random House, 1956.
Rocamora, Agnes, and Anneke Smelik, eds. *Thinking Through Fashion: A Guide to Key Theorists.* London: Tauris, 2016.
Wilson, Elizabeth. *Adorned in Dreams: Fashion and Modernity.* London: Virago, 1985.

Je t'adore à l'égal de la voûte nocturne (extrait) 1857
Charles Baudelaire

Et je chéris, ô bête implacable et cruelle !
Jusqu'à cette froideur par où tu m'es plus belle !

previous spread:
Olivier Theyskens, Fall/Winter 2001–02

left:
Olivier Theyskens, Spring/Summer 1999

right:
Olivier Theyskens, Spring/Summer 2002,
Interview, February 2002

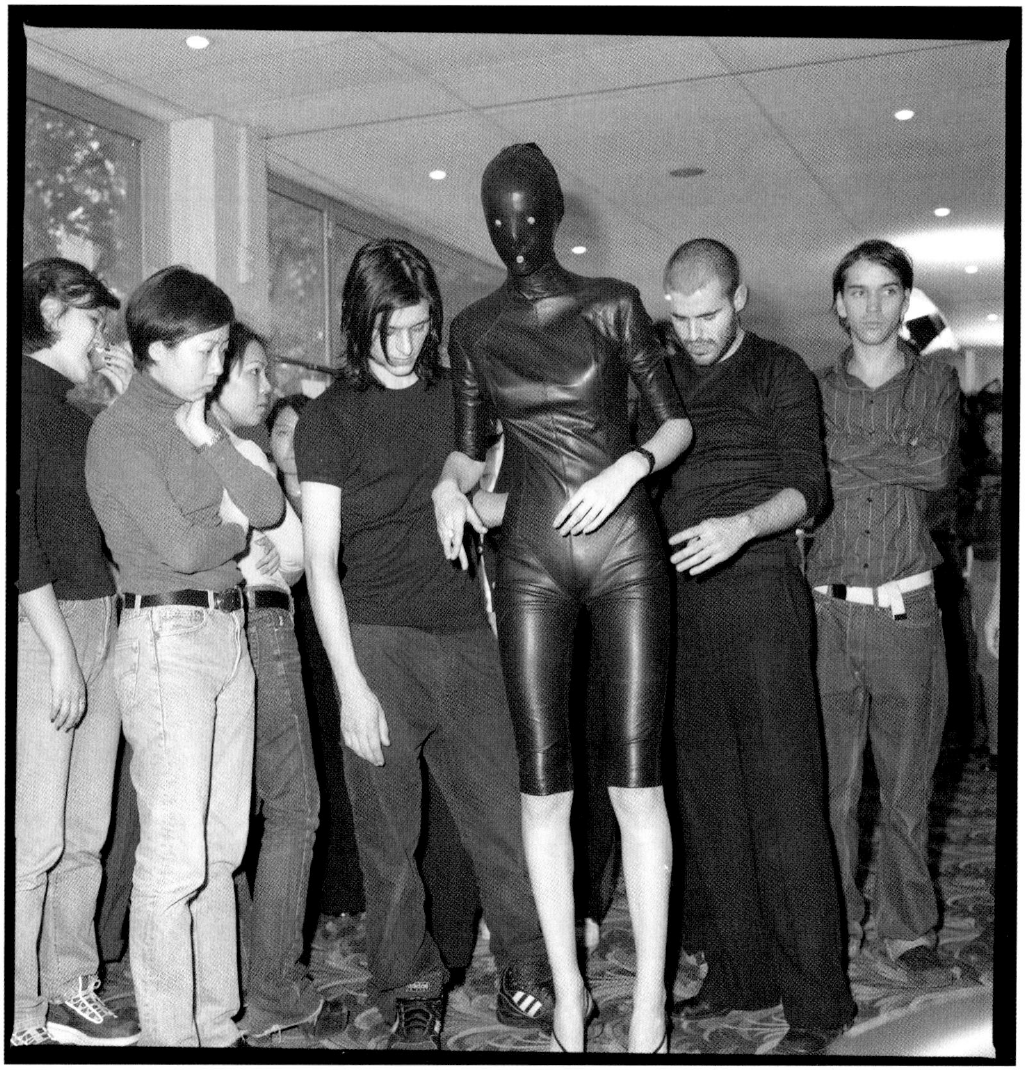

left:
Olivier Theyskens, Fall/Winter 1998–99

right:
Olivier Theyskens, Spring/Summer 1998

following spread:
Olivier Theyskens, Spring/Summer 2002

Rochas

Photographed by Ali Mahdavi
2003–2006

"There is no exquisite beauty ... without some strangeness in the proportion." Edgar Allan Poe

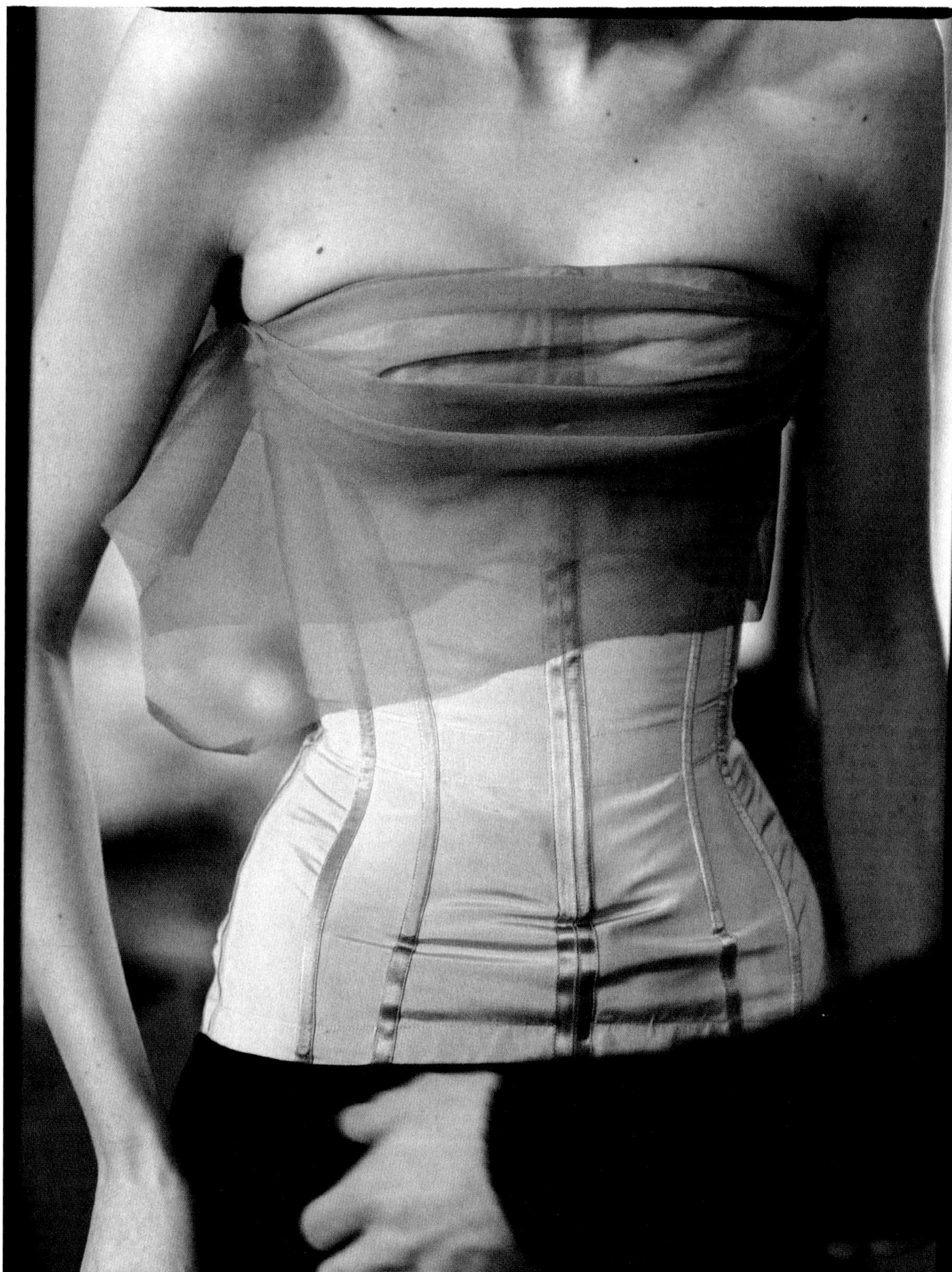

Olivier Theyskens' meeting and subsequent collaboration with photographer Ali Mahdavi was both a happy coincidence, as well as something that seemed inevitable: two artists in search of perfection, both with an eye for timeless beauty and a love of the surreal, simply had to find each another.

They met and began working together in the early years of Theyskens' rise in the world of fashion. Both were enamored of cinematographic light effects, silver gelatin prints, and old-fashioned Hollywood glamour with a surrealistic and burlesque twist.

Ali Mahdavi has investigated and developed the potential of studio photography to its highest refinement, while his pure talent and attention to beauty in the unexpected was also expressed in direct registrations of intimate moments, such as a fitting, or backstage activities at Rochas. His work contributed to the Rochas Woman's new atmosphere of elegance and refinement. His photographs for Rochas, whose play with light and shadow make them at once both sensitive and daring, reinforce the timeless and sometimes surprising beauty of his subjects. By isolating his figures from the often busy backstage surroundings, he increases the intimacy shared between the viewer and the models he photographs.

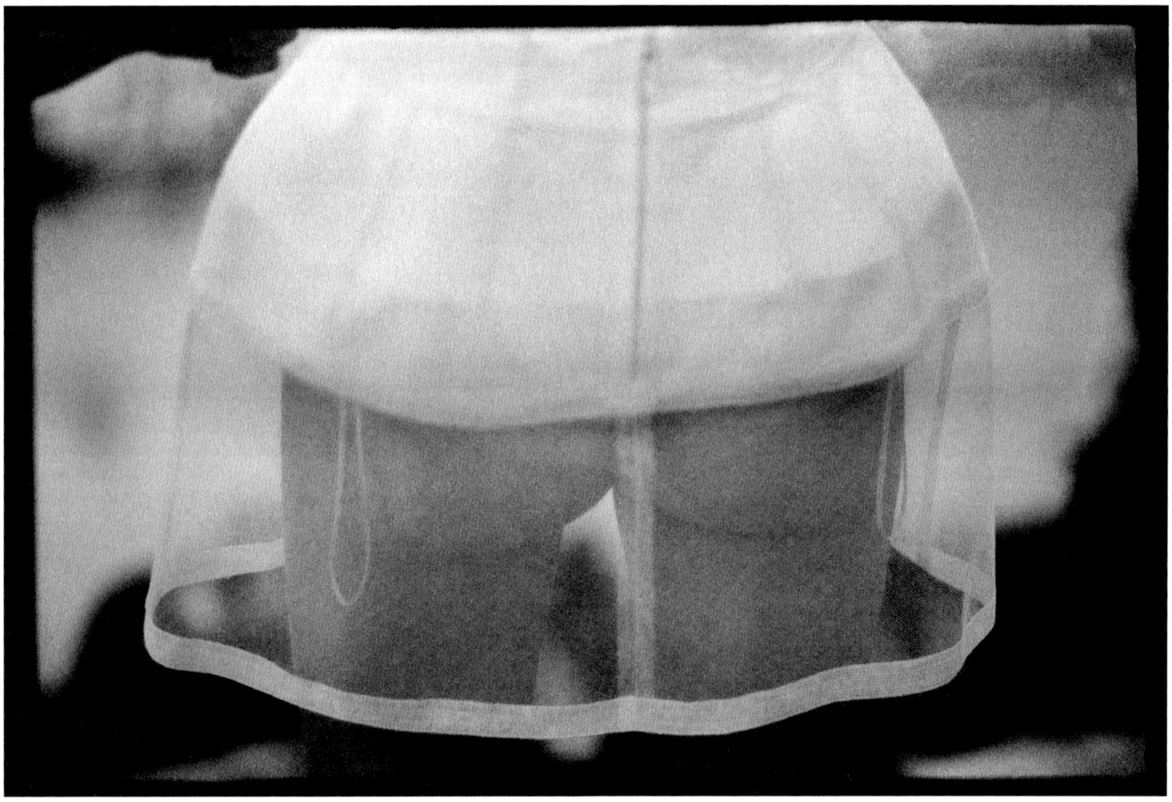

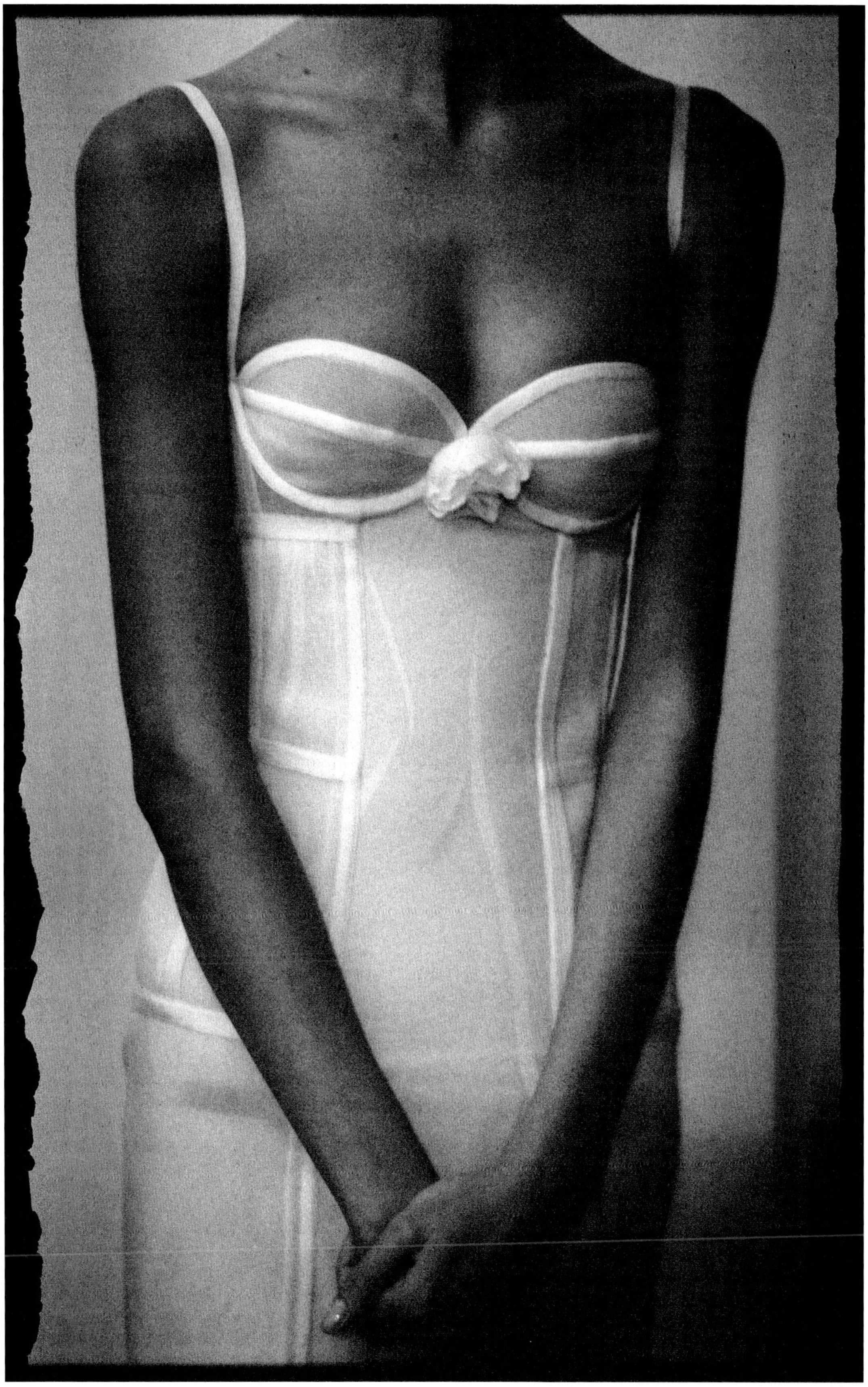

Roulez fleuves du ciel dans nos pétales noirs.
Les ombres ont comblé la terre qui nous porte.
Antonin Artaud : Jardin Noir (1926)

ROCHAS

Genealogy of an Oeuvre

Karen Van Godtsenhoven
Exhibition Curator, MoMu

Olivier Theyskens has a strong personal DNA, but he can also work as a kind of prism for different fashion houses, evoking ever varied atmospheres. Tracing the genealogy of his oeuvre is thus a multilayered exercise: he possesses traits that can place him in a wide range of designer typologies. In terms of schooling, he is self-taught. In terms of method, his heritage is that of the classic couturier. He is a designer who is a draftsman, a designer with a historic sensibility, a second-generation Belgian designer, and a late-twentieth-century designer.

As an autodidact, who - according to at least one teacher - was already formed by the time he started art school (he left after his second year to start his own label), Theyskens can be placed in the category of innovative technical designers alongside Madeleine Vionnet, Charles James, and Rei Kawakubo. With Vionnet, he shares a love for the bias cut, which continues to return in his own label, as well as in his work for other houses (see Olivier Theyskens Spring/Summer 2001 and Fall/Winter 2017-18 and Rochas Spring/Summer 2006), and the technique of direct moulage on the tailor's dummy, a technique that he has been using since he worked for Theory (2010 to 2014) in the United States. With James, he shares an idiosyncratic, constructivist approach and, in the words of his assistant, the fact that "he was born with scissors in his hand." His talent for cut and volume is very visible in his Fall/Winter 1999-00 collection, an early collection reminiscent of the work of both Cristóbal Balenciaga and James, especially in its constructivism. With Kawakubo, he shares unorthodox ideas about the use of materials: in his first collection, he embroidered on plastic and used Toile de Jouy and sheets from the attics of Normandy together with leather and lace; later he incorporated squirrel fur.

Thanks to his well-rounded talents, Theyskens does a great deal of the work himself: drawing, cutting, sewing, draping, and embroidery. Although today's fashion designers usually work as art directors who give out instructions to teams of other designers, Theyskens is predisposed to being a hands-on couturier, one who creates elegance in the spirit of Vionnet, Lucien Lelong, and Balenciaga.

Olivier Theyskens' drawings have an unequalled artistic beauty, as well as a communicative quality, and in today's digital world, there are very few fashion designers who are good at drawing on paper. His exceptional ability to imagine and visualize a collection through drawings that also bring the attitudes and materials to life puts him in a select group of draftsman/designers, such as Christian Dior, Yves Saint Laurent, and Karl Lagerfeld, as well as the heroes of his youth, Christian Lacroix, Thierry Mugler, and Jean Paul Gaultier.

Like Veronique Branquinho, A.F. Vandevorst, Jurgi Persoons, and Raf Simons, Olivier Theyskens is one of a second generation of Belgian designers who caused a furor in Paris in the 1990s. Their collections had a high fin-de-siècle factor, as did the work of British designers Alexander McQueen and John Galliano. With them, Theyskens shares a sense of history, a feel for dark romanticism and references to BDSM. In his case, as memento mori, skulls are more like aesthetic sublimations, where those of McQueen could be called morbid. McQueen, thanks to his use of extreme corsets, has been misunderstood as a designer who objectifies women. Yet neither Theyskens nor McQueen has ever used corsets in the way that Galliano does, with the aim of making women sexually attractive and hence objectifying them for men. Instead, they make constructions in which a woman enjoys her own body and thus objectifies herself for herself. Like McQueen, Theyskens also reveals the artificial character of extremely high heels and a corset: there is no illusion here of a natural woman. The pain of desire is evident, but it can be used, conquered. When you lose yourself in this transgression, the problem of desire resolves itself. The divided female body, marked by Theyskens' characteristic signature of hooks and eyes, becomes a place of protest and joy. Jouissance replaces obedience and objectification.

Theyskens' work also balances on contradictions, for example, the dislocation between modernity and tradition. If we apply the ideas about modernity of important thinkers, such as Baudelaire ("modernity is the transient, the fleeting, the contingent") and Marshall Berman (*All That Is Solid Melts into Air*), to Theyskens' work, we see that the echoes of the past are not historic pastiches, as they are in the work of Galliano or Vivienne Westwood, but instead the transformation of these elements into a contemporary image is avant-garde. Theyskens' concept of time is circular and rejects bourgeois notions about linear time. From the vortex of the past come ever new elements with which he can articulate the present. Like Paul Klee's angel, he is slung from the past to the future, looking behind him as he moves forward. A close reading of Theyskens' fashion history reveals that rare thing in the landscape of contemporary fashion—a wholly original signature.

Olivier Theyskens, Fall/Winter 1998–99,
Catalogue

"To him she seemed so beautiful, so seductive, so different from ordinary people, that he could not understand why no one was as disturbed as he by the clicking of her heels on the paving stones, why no one else's heart was wild with the breeze stirred by the sighs of her veils, why everyone did not go mad with the movements of her braid, the flight of her hands, the gold of her laughter. He had not missed a single one of her gestures, not one of the indications of her character, but he did not dare approach her for fear of destroying the spell."

Gabriel Garcià Marquez – Love in the Time of Cholera (1985)

On this page and the following pages:
Olivier Theyskens, Spring/Summer 2001,
Dutch Magazine #33, May–June 2001

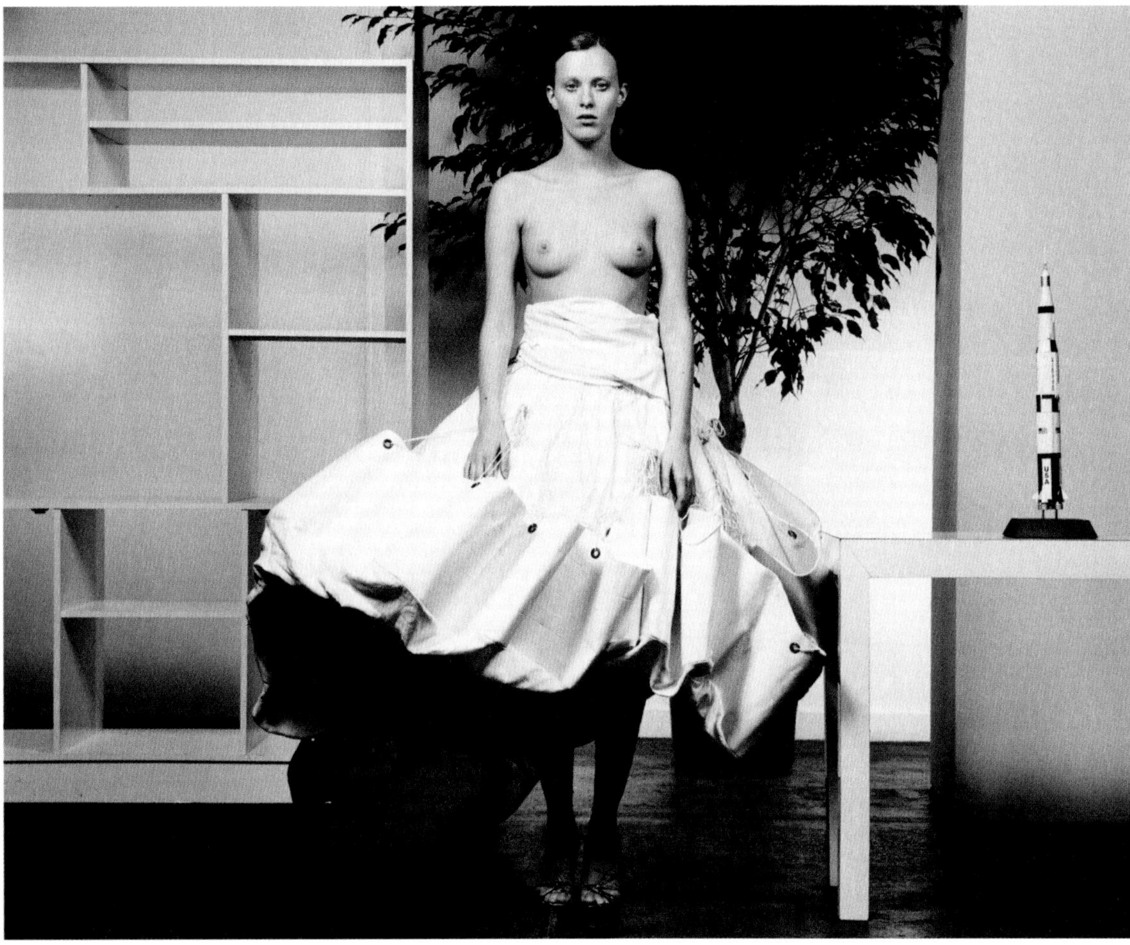

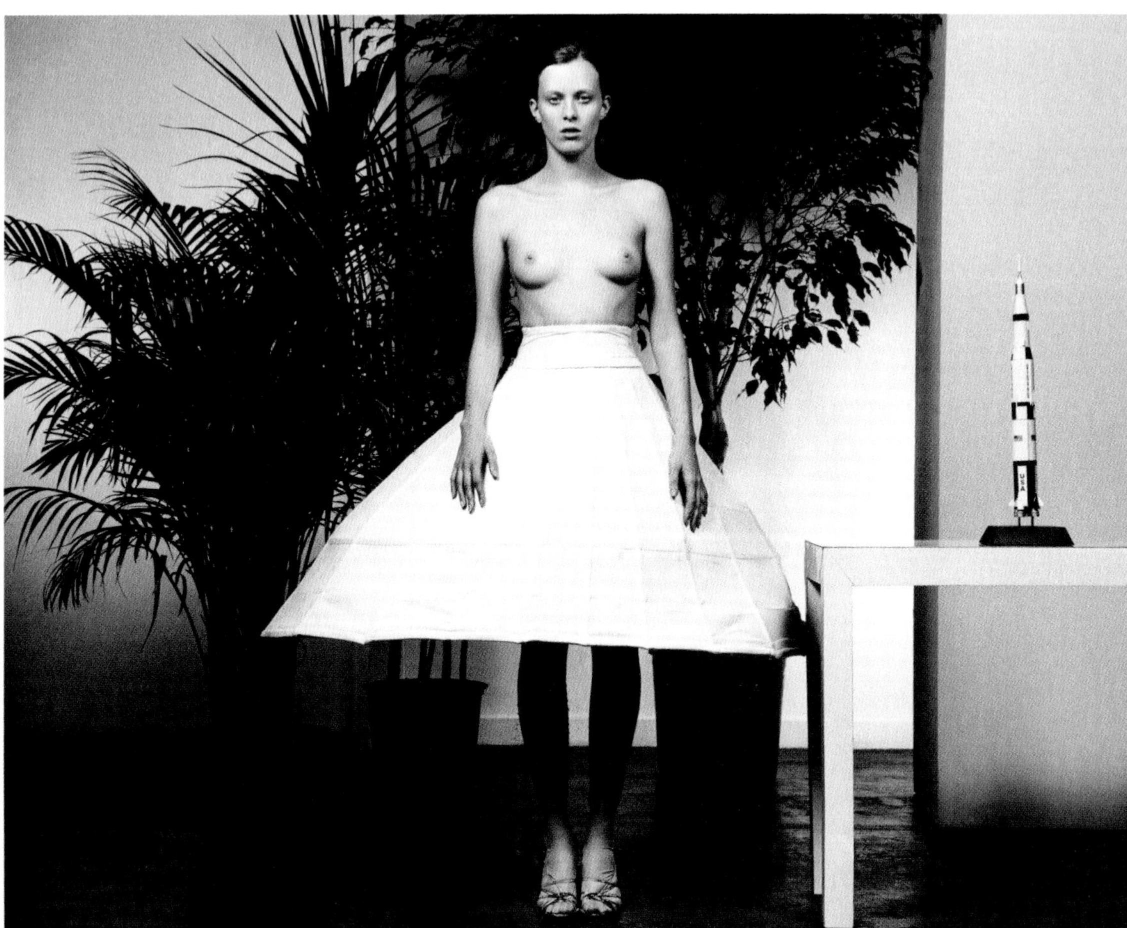

Into the Light

The Trajectory of Olivier Theyskens

Vanessa Friedman,
Fashion Director and Chief Fashion Critic
at *The New York Times*

previous spread:
Olivier Theyskens, Spring/Summer 2017

Rochas, Fall/Winter 2003–04, *Vogue US*,
September 2003

Flip through a series of portraits of the designer Olivier Theyskens over the years and you tend to notice a certain consistency. They tend, for example, to be in black and white. They tend to feature him looking soulfully into the heavens, huge brown eyes fixed on some point perhaps unseen by most mortal men. Often his hair—long and straight, or with a Beatles flop, depending on the date—is used as a sort of scrim to veil a feature or two. Often some form of nudity is involved: a bare, almost concave, chest; limbs twisted around each other in a tortured stance. Mostly, the references are saintly, or prophetic. The import, always, is of fragility: a creature possibly too ethereal for this world.

Or such has been the myth of Theyskens, a designer whose image was forged in the crucible of the late twentieth century, when fashion was teetering on the edge between the jewel-like, family-driven world it had been and the behemoth, brand-driven market-mover it would become. In a way, his story became the story of that transformation; his rise and fall and rise and fall and rise again a metaphor for the battle over the soul of style fought between creativity and commerce that ensued.

Yet, to look at his body of work—to see where he is now and where he has been and how he got there—is to understand that to make such an assumption is to give him less than his due. Theyskens may look like a savior (the Hollywood kind), but he is also a survivor. And his narrative should be seen not as a fable, but as a reality check.

It begins in 1998. After decades in fashion and thousands of collections, there are very few that stand out in the memory—mostly they blur together, an ocean of trends and skirts and styling—but this, I remember. We were in Paris, and rumors had been flying around the sides of runways that some new kid was showing in an abandoned building off the official schedule, and whatever it was, it was going to be worth seeing. Retailers whispered it to editors who whispered it to stylists, and so we went to a dirt-floored warehouse to see a collection of leather hot pants with high-necked sheer Victorian blouses held together by hook-and-eye closures; razor-cut crushed silk jackets over floor-length skirts; corsets and suiting and sweeping ambition. It was a duet between contemporary cool and aggressive historicism that stood out at a time when minimalism and kitsch were the defining aesthetics in fashion. It delivered an emotional gut punch.

Theyskens, then twenty-one, who had dropped out of the Belgian art school La Cambre to start his own brand by the skin of his teeth (and with lace bed sheets donated by his grandmother), was labeled a prodigy: his was fashion's Cinderella story, and he was its Prince Charming, though he was more often deemed the "Prince of Darkness." Madonna wore his gowns twice that year: once to the Oscars (a long black satin coat dress atop a Gaultier tulle skirt) and again to the VH1 Fashion Awards (a canary yellow Elizabethan extravaganza, scarified by hook-and-eye closures along the seams).

He went on to show gowns embroidered with real hair, a bodysuit embroidered with a heart and veins, and shoes topped by stuffed canaries. And as Gucci became Gucci Group and then was bought by Pinault-Printemps-Redoute in the great battle for the brands that took place between it and rival conglomerate LVMH, and designers were thrust into the spotlight as marketable commodities, it was inevitable that Paris would turn its eyes to Theyskens. He had the talent, he had the discovery story, and he looked the part. He was also available: In 2002 he had been forced to close his own brand, after his backer dropped out amid the post-9/11 financial turmoil. Rumors were that Givenchy wanted him in the wake of Alexander McQueen's departure.

But it was Rochas that got him. Theyskens signed with the heritage French house known primarily for its many fragrances (and owned by consumer goods giant Procter & Gamble, which had acquired it when it bought the German hair-care firm Wella in 2003—which happened to own, hidden among all the shampoos, Rochas). Brands from Lanvin to Nina Ricci were enjoying a fashion renaissance via new designers after years of dependence on perfume. Theyskens, with his high romance and high profile—especially among industry power players—paired perfectly with the chic scent of Rochas. Members of the style set held their breath with anticipation.

And then exhaled with glee. Eschewing his darker tendencies, and demonstrating a discernible rigor, Theyskens managed to give the idea of Rochas form; to take the pale pink box and black lace covering of the classic perfume and sculpt it into literal shape. He shrank shoulders and narrowed arms to couture dimensions; added fillips at the hems of little skirt suits and trapeze bustles to the backs of jackets; and almost singlehandedly revived the *jolie madame* cocktail suit. Perhaps the ultimate endorsement came in 2006, when Kirsten Dunst wore an eggshell blue Rochas confection—round-necked, long-sleeved, with a low back and a line that traced her silhouette through the fluted skirt, where a flock of black birds was taking flight—to the premiere of Sofia Coppola's *Marie Antoinette* in Cannes.

It was a telling choice, in many ways, good and bad. The Rochas style, so exacting, so time-intensive—Theyskens did most fittings himself—so expensive, was too let-them-eat-cake. The clothes were too exclusive. There were none of the requisite handbags and shoes (or makeup) that had begun to power the industry.

This was, after all, the age of the accessory. Brands such as Gucci, Chloé, Yves Saint Laurent, and Louis Vuitton had proven that a hit bag—or an it bag—was a crucial component of global success. The margins were so much better than with ready-to-wear, the potential audience so much larger, the possibility of paparazzi snapping a celebrity toting the accessory (and thus providing a free-of-charge ad) so much higher. For a corporate parent whose business was based in the even more accessible world of fragrance, the far horizon and long-term investment demanded by clothing that aspired to the special and unique was too abstruse.

The press christened his collections "demi-couture," which is to say, clothing marked by the painstaking handwork of couture without all the bells and whistles of the atelier. Not quite a decade later, this would actually become a category, with brands such as Schiaparelli relaunched to create exactly these kinds of very limited, special pieces. But in 2006 it was a new idea. And the corporate parent did not know what to make of it. Not long after Cannes, it announced Rochas was up for sale, and then that it was shutting down the fashion division. I remember snagging a little white dress with an iridescent ruffle at the sleeves and hem during a store sale because it felt like a part of fashion history.

But then Nina Ricci smelled opportunity and snapped up Theyskens, unceremoniously ousting designer Lars Nilsson to make room. Nina Ricci was another formerly hallowed French brand that had lapsed into perfume purgatory until it was relaunched by Puig, the Spanish fragrance group with a small division of ready-to-wear names with successful scents (Paco Rabanne, Carolina Herrera).

Once again, fashion clutched its breast. Once again, everyone crowded into the show—this time in an airy tent in the Tuileries Gardens. Once again, the show was memorable: bias-cut knits that swirled around the body with wafting ostrich feathers; cumulus cloud anoraks and gowns that spiraled around the body in foggy shades.

Olivier Theyskens, Fall/Winter 2000–01,
Dutch Magazine #30, November-December 2000

Once again, despite celebrity acclaim and an industry embrace of his tiered gowns, of his red carpet statements cut to the groin in the front and trailing on the ground in the back, it only lasted a short time—in this case three years. In 2009, in the midst of the global economic crisis, Theyskens was forced out to make way for a more market-driven designer. Suddenly, the favored son became a cautionary tale about fashion's dangerous slide on the slippery slope of commerce and the inability of money men to support talent and creativity.

Anna Wintour, the powerful editor of American *Vogue* (and a long-time Theyskens champion), took the unprecedented step of declaring her disgust in the pages of her magazine. "Olivier Theyskens's recent departure from Nina Ricci suggests to me that the vital role of artistic talent has been obscured in the current economic climate," she wrote in the Editor's Letter of the April issue. "My staff and I were shocked to learn that Theyskens's contract would not be renewed; and I am very concerned that the business of fashion is undervaluing the most important asset our industry requires: creative visionaries." Once again it felt like Theyskens has somehow become a symbol of things to come.

In 2010, Alexander McQueen committed suicide. In 2011, John Galliano was fired by Christian Dior after allegedly making anti-Semitic remarks during what was described as a drunken rant and what he attributed to the overwhelming professional pressure he was under. That same year, Christophe Decarnin, who had resuscitated Balmain, was rumored to have suffered a nervous breakdown and left the brand. The industry entered a period of soul searching and mea culpas.

But instead of joining the accusatory chorus, Theyskens did something no one expected: he moved to New York and swapped high fashion for the contemporary world, collaborating with the brand Theory, founded by American Andrew Rosen and a favorite of white-collar women building their wardrobes, on a capsule collection entitled Theyskens' Theory. They seemed an odd couple at first—the Belgian couturier and the Seventh Avenue garmento—but each saw in the other a learning opportunity: for Theyskens, the chance to make clothes his friends could, and would, wear on the street as opposed to simply on special occasions (corduroy flares; sweeping linen trenches; ostrich leather jackets; sharply tailored black suiting); for Rosen, an opportunity to add a bit of European élan and buzz to his basics. After one season, Theyskens became the official creative director of the entire brand. It took the high/low model popular among mass fashion brands such as H&M and posited that it could move from a limited edition marketing-driven single exercise to a potentially long-term strategy.

And though in the end the Theory period lasted only until 2014, when the two parted amicably, it reframed the Theyskens story. When Theyskens returned to Paris to create the first garment under his own name since 2002—a made-to-order wedding dress for Nell Diamond, a personal friend and young American businesswoman, a strapless silk extravaganza embroidered with feathers and sequins finished by a fifteen-foot-long train—it was a statement of belief in the power of singular fashion, but not (despite the cost of the garment) a frivolous one.

I remember having coffee with Theyskens during this interregnum and asking whether he was worried about ever getting another job at a house. He shook his head. But not because he intended to go back on the job market. Because he had come full circle in his own experience.

It was becoming clear that the old days of designers and brands building long-term committed working relationships with each other were, if not entirely over, at least endangered. As designers became chief creative officers, they increasingly became workers for hire and thought of themselves that way. By 2015, job-hopping was the norm at the top of houses, and three years was an average period of employment for a creative director. The only real way to assure longevity of an idea was to put your name over the door, build it slowly, and own it yourself. Otherwise you were just an interpreter, a caretaker, and while it could be a challenging intellectual exercise, the emotional connection was a tenuous one.

Which is how, in autumn 2016, we all found ourselves back in Paris, in a tiny gallery in the Marais, watching the first Olivier Theyskens show in fourteen years. It was small (so is the business)—so small his nearby apartment was the backstage dressing area—and gentle in its ambition. The LBLDs (little black leather dresses) traced by his former trademark hook-and-eye closures, the boned corsetry, the Jane Eyre silhouettes, and the hip-slung trousers together formed a distillation of his history, both creatively and commercially. And it was shown in the afternoon. As was the next collection, unveiled the following February at Le Train Bleu in the Gare du Lyon.

Thus does the journey chug on, in the clarifying light—not of a halo, but of day.

left:
Olivier Theyskens, Fall/Winter 1998–99,
High Fashion Japan, Winter 1998

right:
Olivier Theyskens, Spring/Summer 1998,
"Madonna Chooses Dare," *Spin Magazine*,
April 1998

following spread:
Nina Ricci campaign, Fall/Winter 2007–08

The new creatures — Jim Morrison 1968

She is magician
Female prophet
Sorceress
Dressed in the past
All arrayed.

previous spread:
Theory campaign, Spring/Summer 2014

Theyskens' Theory campaign,
Spring/Summer 2013

"Nothing can be truly replicated. Not a love, not a jewel, not a single line."

Patti Smith, M Train

A Theyskens girl

"I want to speak about style, about allure, about *fashion*..."

Dan Thawley
Editor in Chief, *A Magazine Curated By*,
Contributor for *Vogue* and *Business of Fashion*

Olivier Theyskens for *N°D* Magazine, March 2003

These words epitomize the literal frame of Olivier Theyskens' world—a designer's designer and Renaissance man whose dark fantasy is woven not through intangible dreams but rather the finite realms of cloth. "My love of clothing surpassed my love of costume," says Theyskens, who despite that notion is often remarked as one of the industry's most theatrical designers, whose creations have been worn by icons of the stage and silver screen since the late 1990s. "For me it has always been more about the idea of a beautiful girl in beautiful garments, something much more fashion-based, not just a costume. I loved the idea that the body is clothed beautifully, and that something historical or character-based can take on a new context."

So who is this Theyskens girl? The potent spirit of this ethereal character has floated throughout his career, a shifting paradigm of femininity that is difficult to pin down. Though a sense of nostalgia will always be a quintessential part of Theyskens' oeuvre, his woman has always stood on the brink of another world tinged with retro futurism and an enchanting allure. Her posture, her gaze, and an assumed sensuality have always informed this construction. "My sense of fashion became attached to the muse that I imagined, she has always been her own entity," says Theyskens, reluctant to define her through real-life references, historical or contemporary. "There are a myriad of facets and a whole cast of women and gestures that inform what I do. It would be amiss to name names." That said, his coterie of Belgian models defined the beginning of a "Theysken-ian" era: faces like Kirsten Pieters, Amandine Degré, Hannelore Knuts, An Oost, and Delfine Bafort joined international icons like Stella Tennant, Kirsten Owen, and Karen Elson. They would each help to define Theyskens' clash of '80s and '90s pop culture with his idea of "fin-de-siecle" beauty. This conceit has appeared across the four labels that he has designed—Olivier Theyskens, Rochas, Nina Ricci, and Theyskens' Theory respectively—and with this elusive figure in mind, Theyskens' respect for the canonical history of fashion and its ingrained savoir-faire has embedded even his most daring creations with a classical élan. Perhaps in previous generations you could expect such an earnest, traditional approach from the son of a socialite or aristocrat, born into privilege and surrounded by haute couture. Theyskens, however, had none of that.

"I didn't grow up surrounded by fashion. Like most people, there were no evening gowns in my family, but I discovered fashion from a distance. I was always looking for it and it came to me—my family understood that to spoil me all they had to do was to let me watch Elsa Klensch on CNN, or to come home with a piece of lace or cloth. When I visited my grandmother in Normandy, she would give me these nineteenth century fashion magazines she found at the local markets—these fabulous old "revues" that went all the way back to the 1860s up until the 1930s or so. I still have many of them. For me that was an amazing source of material, as those illustrated reviews were filled with precise drawings of actual pieces. They were also strangely so technical, but there was this element of applied distraction, of women's pastimes for the idle rich. They were filled with instructions and patterns for gowns and embroideries. For me this fed my fantasy to see a sublime outfit in a film, in an opera, or in real life, and to try and understand how they were even made. Ever since, I have the impression that I am on some sort of eternal quest to create pieces today that surpass that sense of beauty and wonder that I had then."

Decades before the digital age, that obtuse exposure to fashion fed Theyskens' love of dramatic silhouette, delicate fabrics, and intricate construction. Swathes of lace, hook-and-eye closures, corsetry and other antiquated details would become the building blocks of his often radical clothes—spliced with black leather and satin, or swimming in delicately destroyed tulle, beading, and feathers. "I feel like my sensibility for fabrics came from the period when I was playing with clothes as a child. I definitely had my favourites: certain swatches, shirts, a fur collar, bits of *broderie anglaise*. I played with textiles in my free time, when I would tie pillows to my waist and layer fabrics over it to create a crinoline, this sort of thing! Another of my obsessions as a child was to watch opera on television, which was always on quite late and so I knew it was the only chance I would have to stay up and watch something until midnight. If it was an opera or a ballet, it was OK. My parents noticed pretty quickly that as long as there were dresses, I was addicted."

If this classicism ever risked to hinder Theyskens' trajectory in fashion, it was the La Cambre school in Brussels that would instill the bold rebellious streak within his work that he has never quite shaken off. "For me the modernity of La Cambre changed my view of fashion," says Theyskens. "It was a time when there were some really incredible people and initiatives that were driving the school. There were people like Billie Mertens, Didier Vervaeren, and Tony Delcampe who had just finished, and as a first year student I really looked up to the work of the graduating students in the fifth year. They opened my eyes to something other than French fashion that was, in my mind at that time, the only voice.

La Cambre taught me to appreciate other forms and expressions of aesthetics. I stopped drawing French girls from the '80s with earrings and all those other old world

Portrait of Olivier Theyskens, *Vogue US*, July 2003

Following spread: Olivier Theyskens for *N°D* Magazine, March 2003

clichés. It must be said that I never really sewed before arriving at La Cambre, but I drew a lot. I was always about the details. On television I would see the illustrations of Christian Lacroix or Yves Saint Laurent, and quite quickly I understood that I could do the same if I wanted. My earliest fashion drawings are from about 1987. But before school, I had never touched a sewing machine. It was only at La Cambre that I even understood a sewing machine had a hidden thread under the fabric—the bobbin thread. I can't even think how many times as a child I tried to use the sewing machine and it would never work as my mother would always remove that thread!"

From this classical place, Olivier's world has expanded across continents and cultures, oscillating between the world of bespoke wedding dresses for high society doyennes to custom creations for the likes of Madonna and the Smashing Pumpkins. One bridal gown, a frothy white Nina Ricci creation, made fashion history (and the pages of American *Vogue*) in 2008 when Theyskens followed it to sunny Cartagena for its debut, where he unceremoniously chopped off its feathered train so that the newlywed Lauren Santo Domingo could dance the night away. Six years later, another Theyskens train made headlines: his wedding gown for New York entrepreneur Nellie Diamond featured a silk satin train that spread five meters wide and required three months of work for its debut in the South of France. The designer sewed it himself after leaving Theory in June of 2014.

Seemingly light years away, Madonna wore Theyskens' lemon yellow "Acidalie" gown to the 1998 VH1 Fashion Awards, (its corseted satin form punctuated with black hook-and-eye like a stitched wound), just as Daphne Guinness, another loyal client, could once be seen striding in Theyskens' heel-less Nina Ricci boots—their swooping construction created a 28-cm void between one's heel and the ground. That these diverse women found natural affinity in Theyskens' work is a testament to his dynamism. How he balances his two worlds of high society and dark glamour has always been Theyskens' strong point—a seductive call-and-repeat of classical tradition and the finesse to rip it apart with indulgent, hedonistic abandon.

Belgitude

Karen Van Godtsenhoven
Exhibition Curator, MoMu

Olivier Theyskens, Fall/Winter 1998–99

"C'était une grande erreur de me faire naître homme,
ça m'aurait beaucoup mieux réussi d'être
mouette ou poisson. Tel quel, je serai toujours
un étranger qui ne se sent chez lui
nulle part, qui ne désire rien vraiment et
que personne ne désire vraiment, qui ne
peut jamais être part de rien, et doit
toujours un peu aimer la mort!"

Eugène O'Neill (1917)

In terms of both his identity as a fashion designer and his artistic affiliations, Olivier Theyskens is very much a Belgian. This is not because of characteristics that might be considered typically Belgian, but because as a Brussels native he carries traits from both the north and the south of the country. In this sense, the absence of a fixed identity, the fluidity of his style, is a Belgian phenomenon. He is someone who grew up on the fault line between French-Roman and Germanic cultures. His work bears typically Belgian contradictions; it is characterized by a melancholy cheerfulness. His girl is adolescent, between childhood and adulthood—she is young, but with an age-old spirit. The atmosphere is both trashy and bourgeois, and his clothes are both the dream of couture and the reality of ready-to-wear. At the crossroads of Europe, we find Olivier Theyskens, a Brussels native with maternal Norman roots, who by Parisian standards will always be an *homme du Nord*, due to his Gothic romanticism, his reserved personality, and his Protestant work ethic (in early interviews, he said he only slept a few hours each night). But to Belgians, he is refined and sensual and someone who, while a fellow countryman, belongs more in Paris than in his native land.

Although Belgian fashion is often identified with the Antwerp school, the fashion landscape in Belgium is very diverse: the Antwerp school is its more northern variation. Olivier Theyskens' fashion identity is not that of Antwerp, but it is Belgian. It combines the rich French tradition of haute couture, with its lavish, body-hugging silk and lace fabrics, and the more modest atmosphere of the north, where wools and linens are basic elements. His sensual tailoring contrasts with the androgynous silhouette of Antwerp, and his creations come more from inner emotion than from an intellectual concept. His mentality is more Catholic than Protestant, with a predilection for the themes of sin and rebirth. His dress with a heart in red lace (Fall/Winter 1998-99) evolved, he told *The New York Times Magazine*, from the idea of a girl "who has so much hidden inside that one day her heart explodes." Theyskens expresses the inexpressible in red lace.

What Theyskens' first collections did have in common with the work of the Antwerp designers of his generation, including A.F. Vandevorst, Jurgi Persoons, and Veronique Branquinho, was a Sadean preference for leather, corsets, and bondage, as well as elements of a gloomy, fin-de-siècle feeling. This was more of a generational sensibility of the 1990s than a geographic phenomenon or a stylistic movement. In his first collections for his own label, we also see an evolution toward more Antwerp-affiliated techniques and materials, such as linen sheets recovered from attics and flea markets by his maternal grandmother in Normandy, as well as more French materials and styles, such as silk, crêpe, and corsetry.

Olivier Theyskens' artistic affiliations—the basis for his intuitive and introverted emotional world—are close to the fin-de-siècle Belgian symbolic artists Léon Spilliaert, Fernand Khnopff, and Félicien Rops. His work carries an implicit message, and his passion for atmosphere and weather conditions as a mirror of the soul is something he shares with Spilliaert: the still tableau reveals what is going on internally. His inspirations are not external affairs, but impressions in line with *la lumière du ciel*. Classic Belgian themes, such as the gray North Sea, a sky filled with clouds, and mussels all appeared early in his career, as well as later in the Theory campaigns. With Rops and Khnopff he shares a magical dream world filled with enigmatic eroticism.

His surrealism is more closely related to the southern surrealism of the Italian fashion designer Elsa Schiaparelli and the Spanish artist Salvador Dalí than with the humorous, surreal game of René Magritte. In his Fall/Winter 1998-99 collections, we see references to the DNA of surrealism: mannequin hands are used as hats (in 1937, Schiaparelli created a hat in the shape of a shoe, inspired by a photograph of Dalí), and embroidered veins are reminiscent of the slits with which Schiaparelli revealed the body under the fabric. The use of hair, (gorilla) fur, and taxidermy as a sexual metaphor in his collections fits into the tradition of surrealist artists, including Meret Oppenheim from Switzerland. In his Spring/Summer 2002 collection, in which miniature dresses created a trompe-l'oeil effect, we nonetheless find elements of the intellectual *détournement* of Marcel Duchamp, with whom Olivier Theyskens shares his Norman roots.

This plate covered with broken mussel shells was part of the stage of the Olivier Theyskens Spring/Summer 2001 show.

following spread:
Olivier Theyskens, Fall/Winter 1998–99

VLADA

Through the looking glass

Theyskens' Wonderland

Elisa De Wyngaert

Curator, MoMu

Nina Ricci

Photographed by Julien Claessens

2007–2009

A December 2003 *Vogue* editorial entitled "Alice in Wonderland" could have just been an aesthetic dress-up party for fashion designers, but as part of the assignment, Annie Leibovitz succeeded in building a picture that revealed the psychological motivations underlying the sensitivity of Olivier Theyskens' visual language. *Vogue* asked twelve fashion designers to imagine their dream Alice dress. In her photographs, Leibovitz played with variations in temperament: a smiling Jean Paul Gaultier as the Cheshire Cat, an expansive John Galliano as the *Queen of Hearts*, and Stephen Jones as the *Mad Hatter*. Theyskens was the exception: in a white shirt and dark jeans, he did not appear to be playing the role of a fictional character. Instead, he appeared in the guise of Lewis Carroll (the pseudonym for Charles Lutwidge Dodgson) the author of *Alice in Wonderland* and a photographer. Daydreaming, Theyskens leaned against the tripod of an old-fashioned camera, while Alice, played by Natalia Vodianova, and as moody as the Victorian girls in Carroll's nineteenth-century portraits, slouches on a chair. The portrait is about more than the voluptuous evening gown from Rochas. It is about Theyskens' love of photography, and it shows him as the creator of the unique world in which his models move. In that world, the models are fresh, youthful *femmes-enfants*. They are Alice.

Theyskens maintains control over everything he creates and presents, but he has allowed two like-minded souls—yet fashion outsiders—to translate his personal universe into photography and fashion shows: portrait photographer Julien Claessens and artist Bernard Tournemenne. The images that have established Theyskens' oeuvre to date go well beyond commissioned commercial photography. Or, as Susan Sontag wrote, "The best fashion photography is more than photographing fashion."[1] Dirk Lauwaert expresses that same idea with his usual intellectual levelheadedness: "The best fashion photographs behave as if they are no longer fashion photographs."[2] Seen through the lens of Claessens, Theyskens' world is indeed no longer just fashion photography. This was not so unusual back in the 1990s, when artists, photographers, and fashion designers pursued creative cross-fertilization in order to suspend the classic split between disciplines. This phenomenon generated iconic duos: Anders Edström immortalized the revolutionary shows of Martin Margiela; Juergen Teller understood the raw realism of Helmut Lang. And from their very first meeting at La Cambre in 1995, Claessens was able to capture Theyskens' world in atmospheric images.

In times of immediacy, of Instagram and live streaming, this duo became digital counter-revolutionaries in their analog search for beauty and fragility. In this, Annie Leibovitz was something of a visionary: thirteen years after her "Alice in Wonderland" editorial, Theyskens and Claessens experimented with a collodion camera from 1859 for their *Balade Ephémère* series. That wet-plate photography (created with assistance from Nicolas Lambert of Studio Baxton in Brussels) was precisely the same method employed by Lewis Carroll. Using it, they created life-size portraits of girls in the Belgian countryside dressed in pieces from Theyskens' Spring/Summer 2017 collection. The slowness (one image per hour at the most, as compared to the average of 500 to 3,000 images captured per day using digital photography) and the unpredictability (images will fail) of that process fascinated them. Their shared sensitivity to the soul of the image brought them back to the early years of the medium. For Theyskens' oeuvre, Claessens favors black-and-white photography, because it has an emotional and erotic singularity. He believes it invokes a nostalgic feeling for "what has been." As Claessens explains in 2017, "Olivier and his work have something romantic, nostalgic about them. Even if he uses highly technical materials and if the tailoring in his clothes has great modernity, I cannot stop myself from thinking of the past when I see what he makes." Theyskens' world is full of contrasts: historically inspired silhouettes in futuristic materials, a modern collection seen through the lens of a Victorian camera.

During the fashion shows, for backstage photography, Claessens exchanges his analog Hasselblad for a digital camera in order to (more quickly) capture the right moment: backstage is depicted through the eye of a portrait photographer. The images are not journalistic or anecdotal, not attempting to be fashion images, not created with an eye to making clothing attractive or illustrating details and finishing. Instead, these images are filmic, dark, and surreal, yet without narrative. Here, Theyskens' models are lonely figures, lost in their thoughts and exhibiting inexplicable tranquility in the hectic behind-the-scenes environment. Claessens captures alien movements and expressions that others would fail to notice. These are images that invoke nostalgia for the moments in which they were frozen. The photographs of the girls wearing Theyskens' collections seem to be memories from our subconscious, and in them time, therefore, becomes indefinable.

Theyskens is not a storyteller, such as Jean Paul Gaultier or John Galliano, nor is he a minimalist, such as Jil Sander or Helmut Lang. Like the photographs, his fashion shows are a world unto themselves. His first show, *Gloomy Trips* (Fall/Winter 1998-99), was an atmospheric masterpiece with pale models who disdainfully walked past the audience against a background of cries of pain and aggressive flashes of light. Tournemenne, always at Theyskens' side during shows, described that first show as chaotic, because too many people had come to see it. That chaos was, in fact, more than outdone by the small, yet meaningful interventions of light and sound. The atmosphere was poetically claustrophobic, disturbing, and hypnotic.

In Theyskens' shows, the models might walk under a bank of clouds (Spring/Summer 2000), or cross a catwalk covered with mussels (Spring/Summer 2001). They might appear from a misty emptiness (Fall/Winter 2000-01) or out of a dark wilderness (Nina Ricci, Fall/Winter 2007-08). In the years when he was working for Rochas and Nina Ricci, the scenography was conceived on an architecturally larger scale, but the principle remained consistent. With just a minimal set design, the shows became atmospheric experiences with stimuli for the senses. For years, Tournemenne has observed that Theyskens is something of a god for women, and he muses about the intimate synergy between the designer and the models. Theyskens insists on a link between a silhouette and a model—it may be friendship, or just a feeling. With his encyclopedic memory for every single one of his shows, he still knows the name of every model and the particular look she wore. Because there is no fixed narrative, it is unclear what the girls who appear on the catwalk (from that dark wilderness or misty emptiness) themselves experience. Who are they? Nymphs, queens, figures from the underworld? Are they sensitive, traumatized, or malicious? The imagination of the viewers is duly sparked by their appearance, just as it is by the backstage photography Claessens produces.

You traverse the apparently impenetrable world of Olivier Theyskens through images that succeed in capturing those moments of estrangement, moments that others simply pass by. His fashion shows are performative translations of his thoughts. In a frozen image, and in the few fleeting moments of a fashion show, the visual language of Claessens and Tournemenne helps reveal Theyskens' inner world. In that language without words, the viewer also briefly becomes an author.

1 Susan Sontag, *On Photography* (London: Penguin Books, 1977).
2 Dirk Lauwaert, *Lichtpapier: teksten over fotografie* (Antwerp: Fotomuseum Provincie Antwerpen, 2007), 85.

VLADA

LINDSAY
4
5

JILL B
6

Visions on Paper

Karen Van Godtsenhoven
Exhibition Curator, MoMu

Olivier Theyskens,
Fall/Winter 1999–00

Olivier Theyskens,
Fall/Winter 1999–00

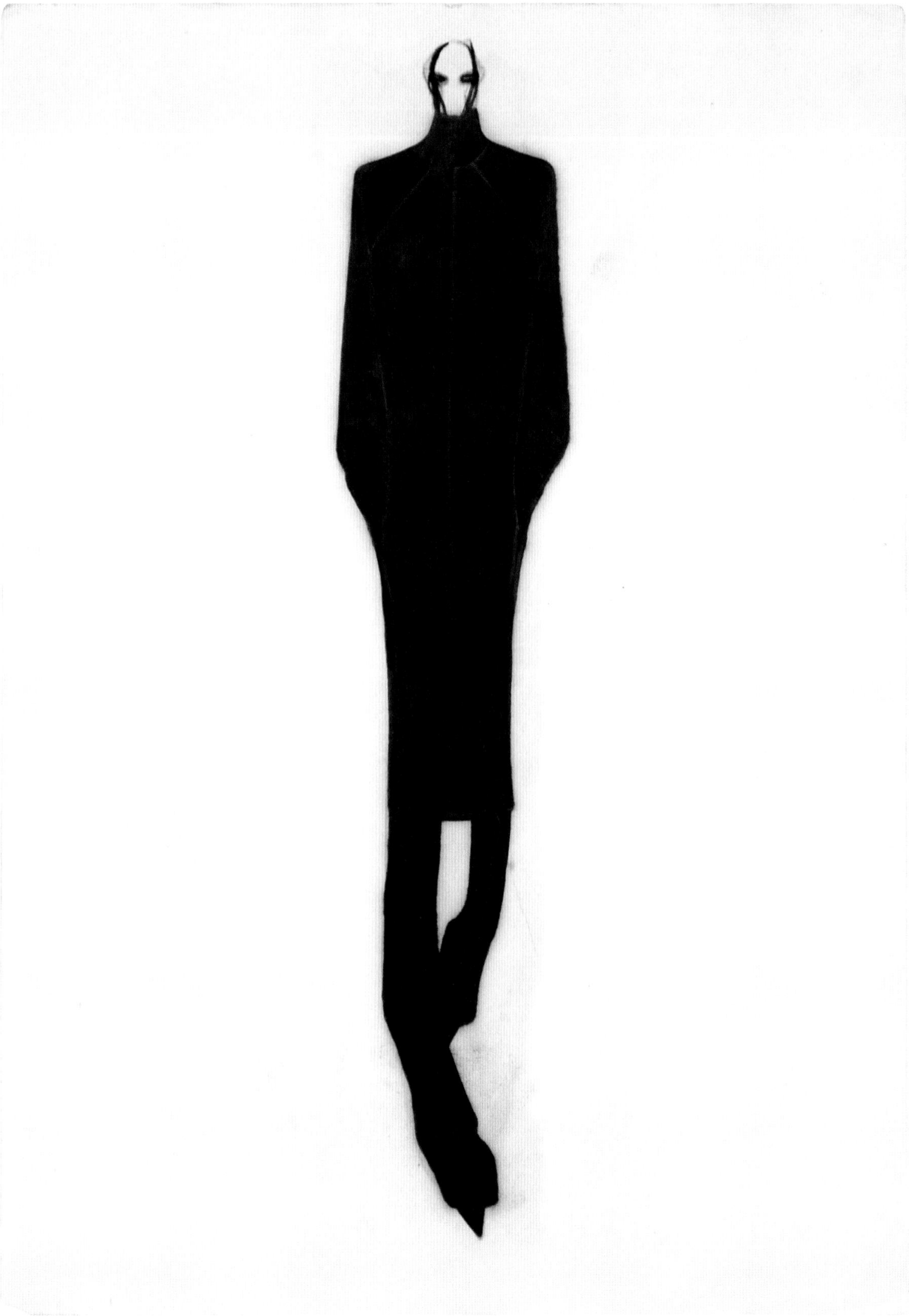

"We had never had a student who was so mature and accomplished, right from the start, as Olivier," says Francine Pairon, founder of La Cambre's fashion department and Theyskens' former teacher. "He was so young—we had no idea where it came from. This had to be an old soul, an *ancien esprit*."

Indeed, Olivier Theyskens had an innate drawing talent. His gift and predilection were so great that graphic design and fine arts instructors at La Cambre, where he studied, attempted to entice him away from the fashion department. But he was not at all interested in going through life as a fine artist: his alternative to fashion was architecture. He is interested in building volumes and "houses" for the body. His drawings, in addition to being aesthetic, are also functional. They communicate the dream and the idea. In his own words, "The intention of the garment is important. That comes first, and then come the commentary and fabric samples for the studio." The designer's illustrations are the platonic ideal that the actual article of clothing hopefully will meet. "It is always dangerous to go from two-dimensional to three-dimensional. Sometimes the two-dimensional is more aesthetic, and the three-dimensional is not." His drawings are an example of Marcel Proust's *mémoire involontaire*, an image from the subconscious that comes to the fore on paper.

Olivier Theyskens does not make narrative mood boards; rather he creates a world through his illustrations. For every collection he adopts a somewhat different graphic style, atmosphere, and attitude, as well as a different color palette.

Theyskens' consciousness is expressed in his drawings, as are his ideas. Those ideas appear on paper, in sequence, covering what will ultimately become the fashion show, illustrated with fabric samples and Polaroids. Technically, the drawings are so complete that they serve as a working instrument, ready to give the show lineup its form. After a few seasons, there was an evolution from a static, frontal image to a three-quarter profile view where the fluidity of the fabrics, the fall of light, and the three-dimensional forms became clear. Olivier Theyskens is very gifted with scissors and drapery techniques, but he still expresses himself with ink, paint, pencil, and marker. Many hours of work resulted in beautiful textures and shapes. He now has a collection of perfectly organized boxes filled with drawings, a life's work that includes all of his collection illustrations from 1998 to 2009. Until he began working for Theory, the most important work for a collection was done when the drawings on paper were complete: the real creation took place on paper.

"I saw the drawing as a part of the work I was contracted to deliver for the house; when my drawings were ready, the collection was ready," he says. The subsequent treatments of prints and textiles were exceptionally true to the drawings. The drawings themselves sometimes resemble paintings by René Gruau, which in turn responded to the increasingly industrial and mechanical character of fashion illustrations and magazines in the latter half of the twentieth century. But Olivier Theyskens is by no means ill-disposed toward digital media. When he began working with the Theory label in the United States in 2010, he made his drawings on his iPad. Those drawings were purely technical and functional; then they all but disappeared, because Theory worked more directly from tailors' dummies.

Olivier Theyskens draws the body in clothing. The girls who populate his collections are the dream models for his silhouettes. Together, they form an idea. It is a modern idea that it is not only the woman who is desired, as Charles Baudelaire and Gustave Flaubert wrote, but her adorned, clothed body. The illustration connects the living body with non-living fabric. In addition to the clothed body, thanks to its style and movement, not to mention its attitude, the drawings encompass *l'air du temps*, the mystery of fashion. Olivier Theyskens' vision lives on paper.

Olivier Theyskens,
Fall/Winter 1999–00

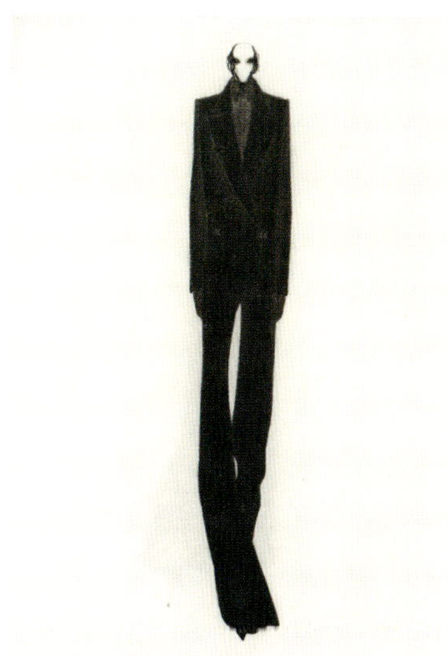
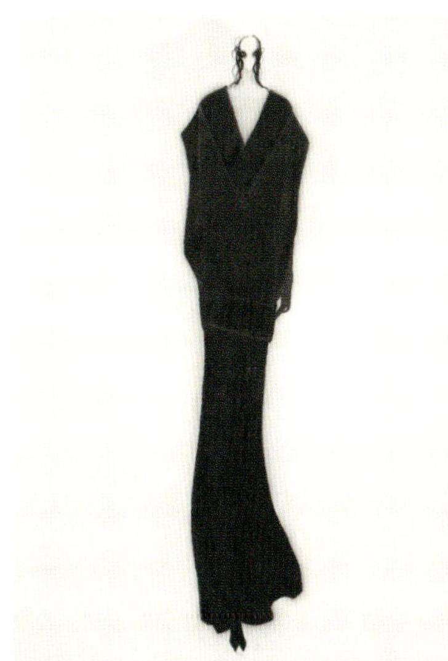

Olivier Theyskens,
Fall/Winter 1999–00

Olivier Theyskens,
Fall/Winter 2000–01

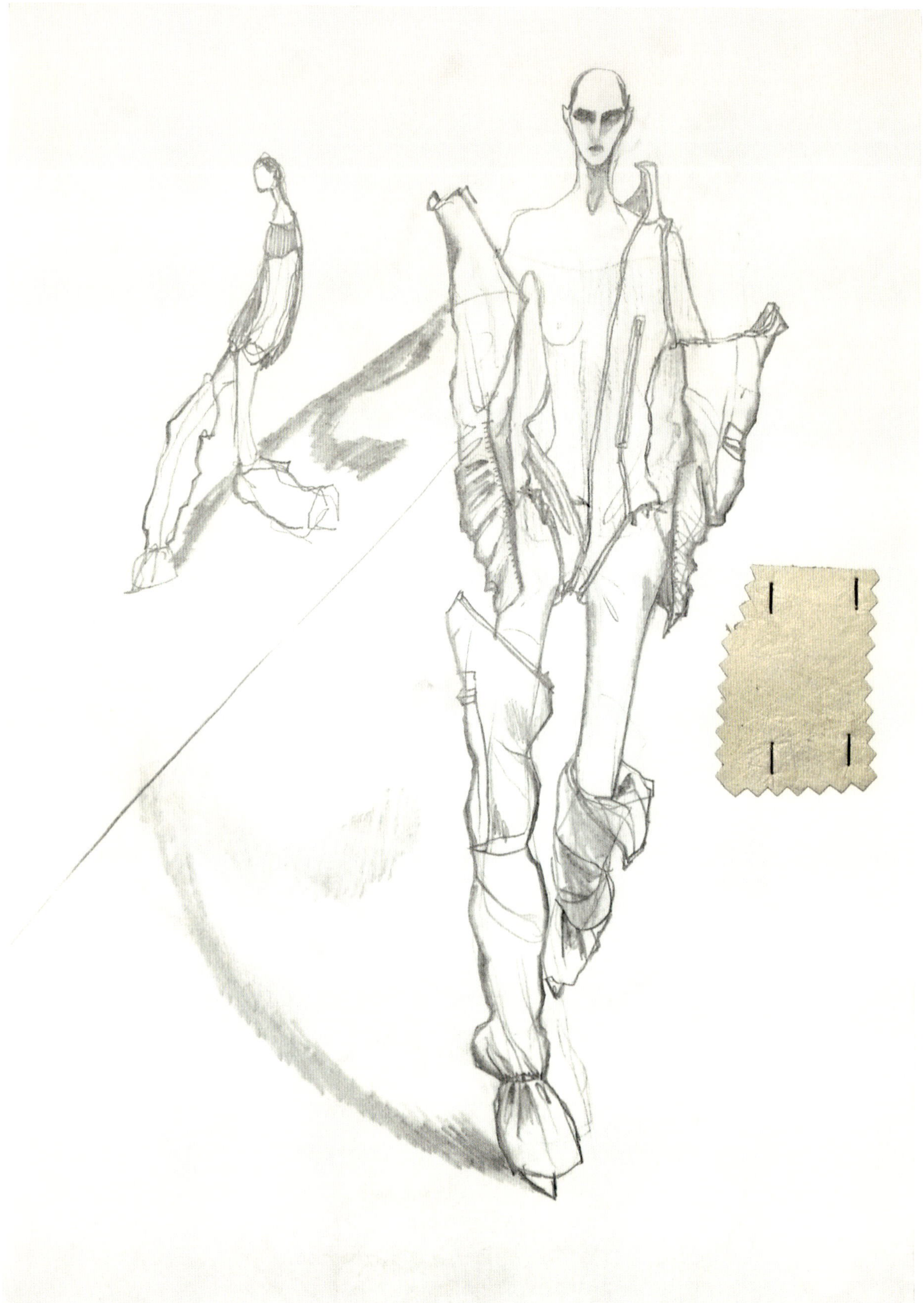

Rochas,
Fall/Winter 2003–04

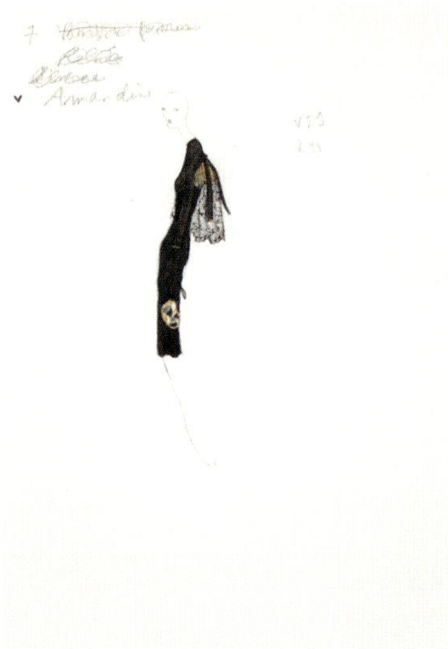

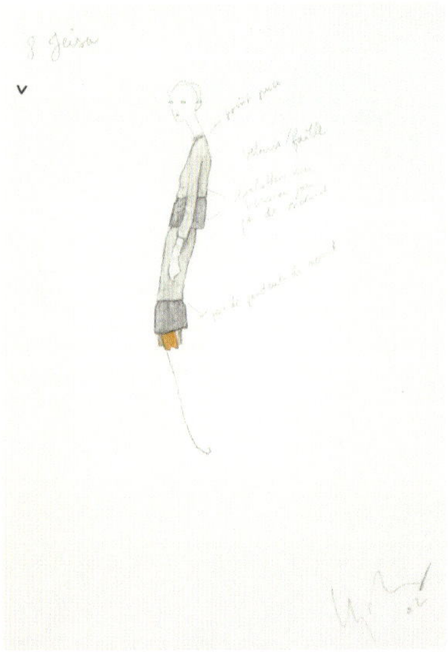

Rochas,
Fall/Winter 2003–04

Rochas,
Fall/Winter 2003–04

28 Kim Noorda

Rochas,
Spring/Summer 2004

Rochas,
Fall/Winter 2004–05

Olivier Theyskens,
Spring/Summer 2001

Olivier Theyskens,
Spring/Summer 2002

Nina Ricci,
Fall/Winter 2007–08

Olivier Theyskens,
Spring/Summer 1999

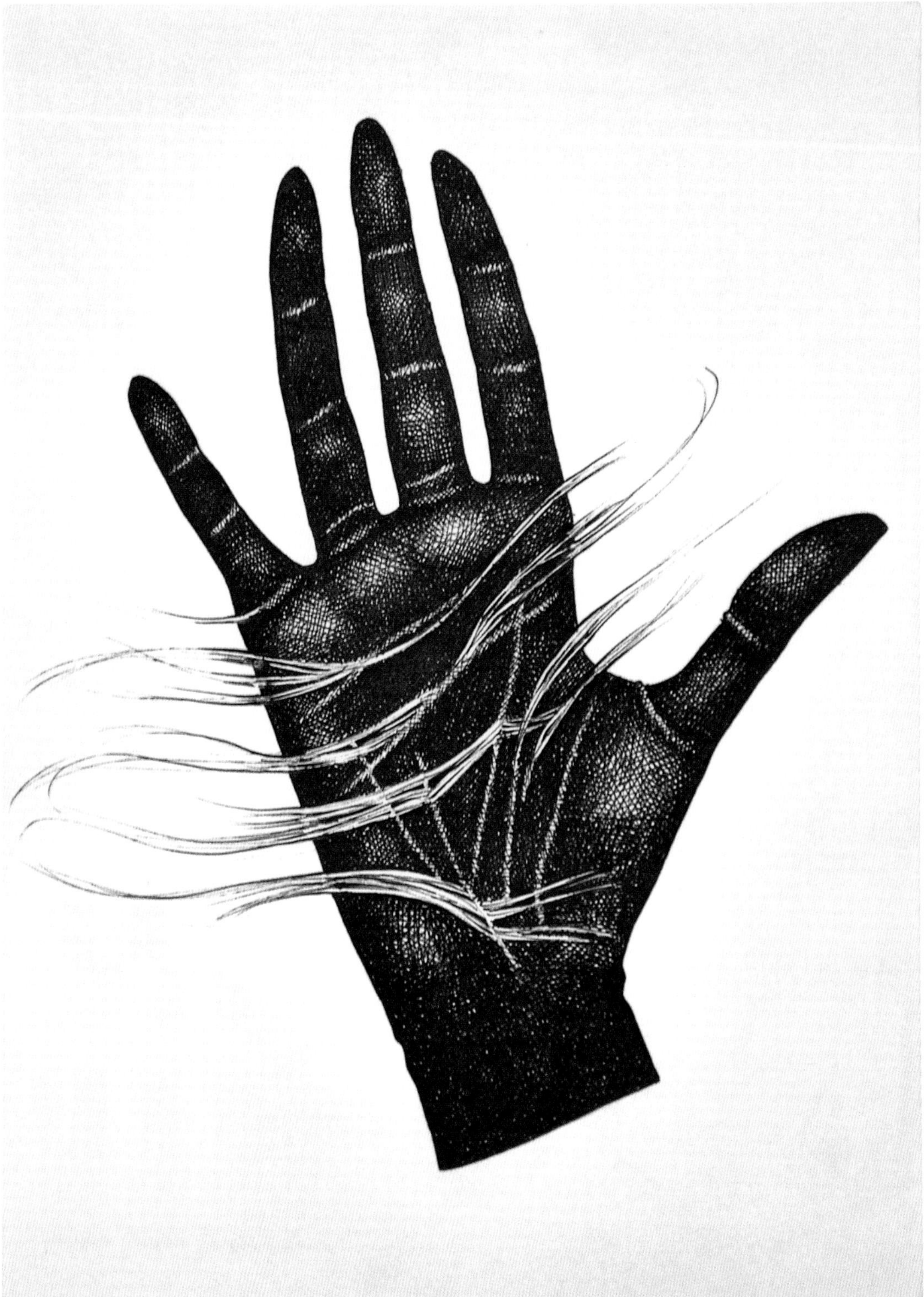

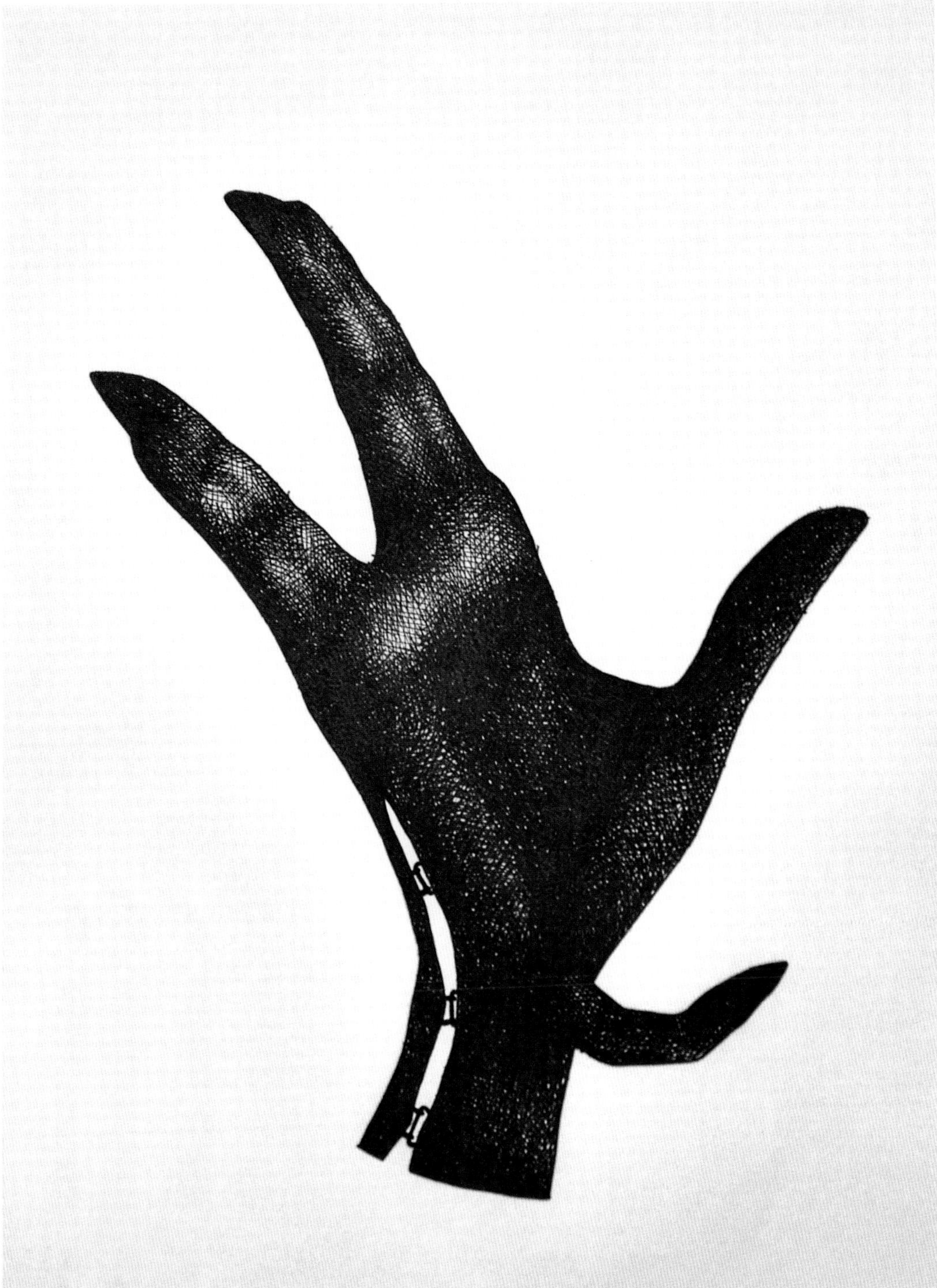

Olivier Theyskens,
Spring/Summer 2000

Olivier Theyskens,
Spring/Summer 1999

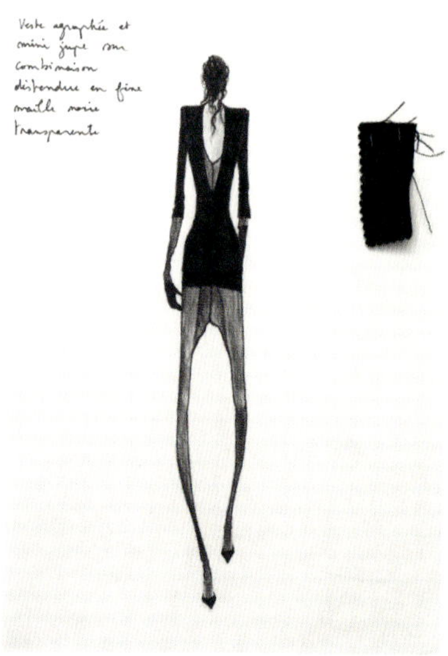

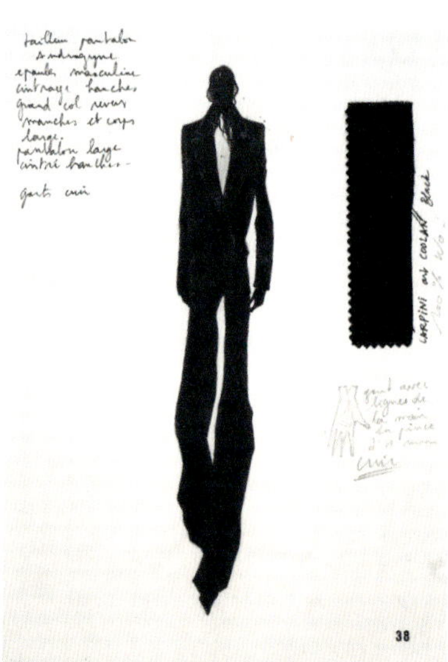

longue et volumineuse
robe noire dont
l'ouverture en forme
de croix est agraphée
+ gants noirs en cuir
GUILLAUD
popeline moirée
art 4800/R205
col 99

Olivier Theyskens,
Spring/Summer 1999

31

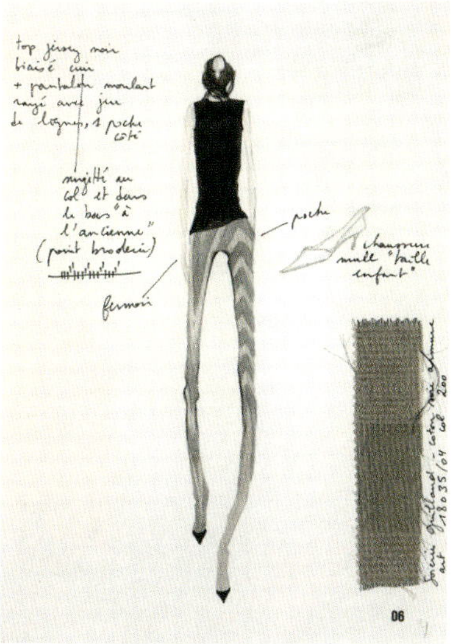
06

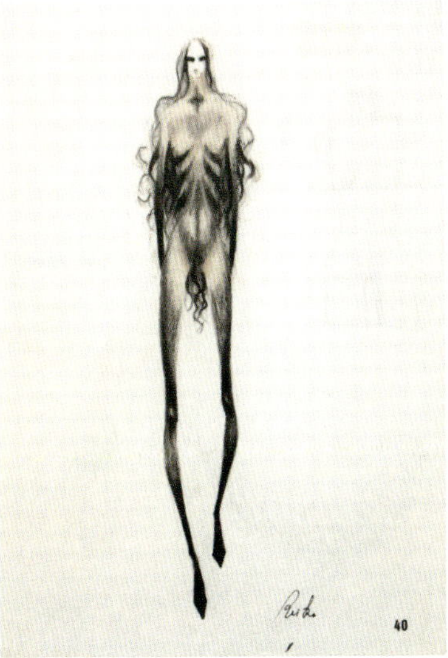
40

Nina Ricci,
Spring/Summer 2009

print = Look 9/11
variante A

Nina Ricci,
Spring/Summer 2009

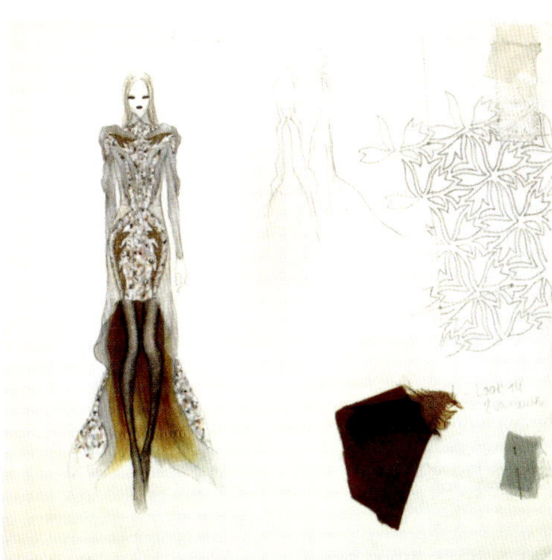

Rochas,
Spring/Summer 2006

Olivier Theyskens,
Fall/Winter 1998–99

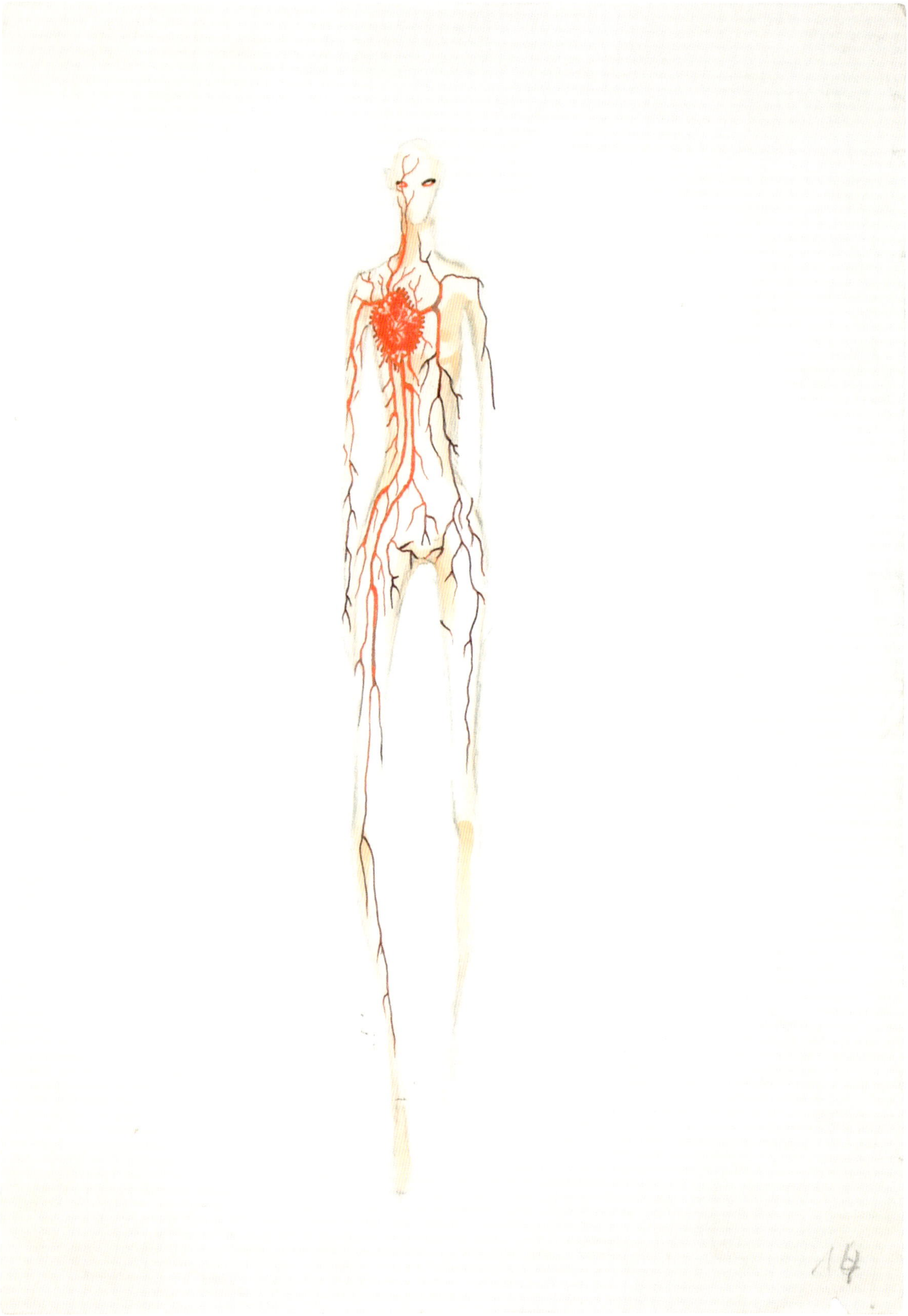

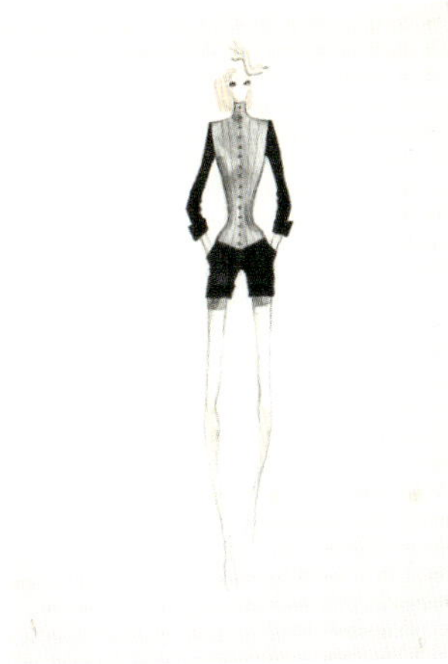

Nina Ricci,
Fall/Winter 2009–10

KARLIE KLO
NE
XT

Nina Ricci,
Fall/Winter 2009–10

Following pages: Olivier Theyskens,
Spring/Summer 2017

ANASTASIJA
KONDRATJEVA
elite

IRINA
KULIKOVA

RIEN ?
JLIANA
TIKHOVA
elite

LILY
DONALDSON

MAGDALENA
FRACKOWIAK
elite

SIGRID
AGREN
elite

CONTENTS

EXHIBITION

This publication accompanies the *Olivier Theyskens: She walks in beauty* exhibition at the MoMu Fashion Museum in Antwerp, taking place from October 12, 2017 through March 18, 2018.

This exhibition is presented through the auspices of the Provincial Council of the Province of Antwerp.

GOVERNOR FOR THE PROVINCE OF ANTWERP
Cathy Berx

PROVINCIAL REGISTRAR OF ANTWERP
Danny Toelen

MEMBERS OF THE EXECUTIVE BOARD
Luk Lemmens
Ludwig Caluwé
Inga Verhaert
Bruno Peeters
Peter Bellens
Rik Röttger

HEAD OF THE DEPARTMENT OF CULTURAL INSTITUTIONS
Walter Rycquart

CURATORS
Karen Van Godtsenhoven, with Lydia Kamitsis

EXHIBITION DESIGN
Glenn Sestig

WITH SPECIAL THANKS TO:
Olivier Theyskens
Agnès Magoga
Bernard Tournemenne
Team Olivier Theyskens
Julien Claessens & Thomas Deschamps
Arianne Phillips
Luciano de Medeiros
Gino Beeckman

MOMU — MODEMUSEUM PROVINCIE ANTWERPEN/FASHION MUSEUM ANTWERP
DIRECTOR
Kaat Debo

CURATORS
Elisa De Wyngaert
Karen Van Godtsenhoven

PRODUCTION MANAGER
Robby Timmermans, with Justin Vanneste

PRESS & COMMUNICATION
Leen Borgmans
Gabriëlle De Pooter
David Flamée

CONSERVATION & MANNEQUINS
Frédéric Boutié
Danique Klijs
Ellen Machiels
Wim Mertens
Kim Verkens

PUBLIC RELATIONS
Klaartje Patteet

WITH SPECIAL THANKS
The MoMu team, volunteers and interns

LENDING MUSEUMS
Musée des Arts Décoratifs, Paris, *Pamela Golbin*
Musée de la Mode Palais Galliera, *Alexandre Samson, Corinne Dom*

PRIVATE LENDERS
Julien Baulu
Hamish Bowles, Molly Sorkin & Jennifer Park
Ariel De Ravenel
Naura Keiser
Agnès Magoga
Nina Ricci, Antoinette Gendre
Rochas, Nathalie Prevoteau
Valeria Pesci
Stéphane Subrenat
Theory, Siddharta Shukla
Olivier Theyskens

Mannequins in the exhibition are provided by
Bonaveri Mannequins: Tribe

CATALOGUE

MARKED

MARKED is an initiative of Lannoo Publishers
www.marked-books.com

Join the MARKED COMMUNITY
- @booksbymarked

Register on our MARKED newsletter at www.marked-books.com to regularly receive our newsletter with information about new books on art, design, interior, fashion, photography, food and travel, as well as interesting, exclusive MARKED offers and events.

Authors: Kaat Debo, Elisa De Wyngaert, Vanessa Friedman, Lydia Kamitsis, Wim Mertens, Dan Thawley & Karen Van Godtsenhoven

Translation and Editing: Irene Smets

Graphic Design: Philippe Galowich in collaboration with Maxemilian Nilsson and Louison Coulom

Cover: Hannelore Knuts in Olivier Theyskens for Nina Ricci Fall/Winter 2007-08, Encens magazine, © Sybille Walter

Back cover: Olivier Theyskens Spring/Summer 1998 © Jurgen Rogiers

Image Research: Monica Ho, Clara Runge, Karen Van Godtsenhoven

For Rizzoli International Publications:

Translation from Dutch into English: Mari Shields

Translation from French into English: Denise Jacobs

Project Editor: Jennifer Duardo

English Copy Editor: Natalie Danford

English Typesetting: Kayleigh Jankowski

Provincie Antwerpen

MODEMUSEUM

Vlaanderen
verbeelding werkt

PHOTOGRAPHY CREDITS

Julien Claessens & Thomas Deschamps 6-85
Pascal Demeester 87, 90, 92, 105, 204-205
Inez Van Lamsweerde & Vinoodh Matadin/Courtesy Gagosian 91, 179
Deborah Turbeville 93
Jurgen Rogiers 94-95, 125
Julien Claessens 96, 103, 108, 168-169, 206-217
Diego Uchitel 99
Les Cyclopes - Damien Bénéteau & Xavier Cariou 101, 133, 163, 189, 192-193
Steven Meisel/Art + Commerce 107
Etienne Tordoir 112-113, 199, 202-203
Michel Damanet 115
Marleen Daniëls (Asst. Bert Houbrechts) 116-117
Michel Haddi 120-121
Lothar Schmid/Elle/Scoop 123
Yannis Vlamos/Pixelformula 127
Ali Mahdavi 128-129, 137-159
Archive Olivier Theyskens 130, 134-135, 160-161, 198, 219-265
Karl Lagerfeld 131
Jean-François Carly 132, 195
Thomas Schenk 164-167, 174-175
Irving Penn 171, 191
Ronald Stoops 178
Annie Leibovitz 180-181
Lachlan Bailey 182-183
Willy Vanderperre 184-185
Julien Claessens/Thomas Deschamps & Baxton Studio 186-187, 196
Christoph Klenzendorf/Totem Girault 200-201
Gio Staiano 266-267

MODEL CREDITS

Madonna 91, 179
Audrey Tchekova, Kasia Pysiak 93
Amandine Degré, Kirsten Pieters 95
Natalia Vodianova 99
Linda Byrne 101
Lily Cole 107
Colette Pechekhonova 112
Malin Persson 113
Unknown 115, 118
Eva Strus 117
Audrey Tchekova 123
Kirsten Pieters, An Oost 125
Kirin Dejonckheere 127, 196
Tamara Cesnovar 128-129
Jen Dawson 130
Nicole Kidman 131, 171
Mathilde 133
Madeleine Blomberg 137
Eugenia Volodina 140, 142
Erin Wasson 145
Gemma Ward 149, 157
Hana Soukupova 151
Elise Crombez 152
Lily Donaldson 158
Anne-Catherine Lacroix 160
Amandine Degré 163
Karen Elson 164-167, 174-175
Kirsten Pieters 178, 195, 204-205
Anabela Belikova 180-181
Stella Tennant 182-183, 203
Wylie Hays 185
Femke Vershelden, Kirin Dejonckheere 186-187
Lisa Lauwaert 199
Kasia Pysiak 200
Nina Heimlich 202
Suvi Koponen, Uliana Tikhova, Irina Kulikova, Kim Noorda 206
Kelli Lumi, Kasia Struss 211
Amanda Laine 212-213
Uliana Tikhova, Irina Kulikova, Kim Noorda, Kendra Spears, Anabela Belikova 215
Tanya Dziahileva 216-217

First published in the United States of America in 2018 by Rizzoli Electa, a division of Rizzoli International Publications, Inc.
300 Park Avenue South • New York, NY 10010
www.rizzoliusa.com

Originally published in Dutch in 2017 by Lannoo

2018 2019 2020 2021 / 10 9 8 7 6 5 4 3 2 1
ISBN: 978-0-8478-6246-7
Library of Congress Control Number: 2017949657
Printed in the Netherlands

#AREYOUMARKED